The Essence of George Fox's
Journal

The Essence of George Fox's *Journal*

Edited with an Introduction by
Hunter Lewis

The Essence of . . . series of books are edited versions of great works of moral philosophy, distilled to reveal the essence of their authors' thought and argument. To read the complete, unedited version of this work, and see the excised passages, please visit our website at www.AxiosInstitute.org.

Axios Press
P.O. Box 118
Mount Jackson, VA 22842
888.542.9467   info@axiosinstitute.org

Library of Congress Cataloging-in-Publication Data

Fox, George, 1624–1691.
[Journal of George Fox]
The essence of George Fox's Journal / edited with an introduction by Hunter Lewis.
p. cm.
Includes index.
ISBN 978-1-60419-053-3 (pbk.)
1. Fox, George, 1624-1691—Diaries. 2. Quakers—Great Britain—Diaries. 3. Quakers—Great Britain—History—Sources. I. Lewis, Hunter. II. Title.

BX7795.F7A3 2012
289.6092--dc23
[B]

2011047058

Contents

Introduction

GEORGE FOX FOUNDED the Religious Society of Friends, better known as Quakers, a form of Christianity which has had an immense influence on religious thought throughout the world, and which also played a large role in the early days of the American colonies.

Friends rely on orthodox Christian scriptures, but otherwise lack a formal creed. They believe that Jesus speaks to each of us directly, through personal revelation, which takes the form of an inner voice. This has been called a form of mysticism, but at least initially it accepted scripture as an unimpeachable authority, and it did not lead its adherents to a monkish withdrawal from the world, but rather to just the opposite: a spirited engagement in everyday life, along with a very active proselytizing of the world.

This proselytizing was energetic and utterly fearless, but it was also pacifist, just as Jesus was. The rules forbade any violence, even self-defense, and certainly any military service. A Christian life above all emulated Jesus's. It should be simple and consist of good works and honorable service. It should not be apart from one's faith, but directly reflect it.

A Quaker's life was also a shared life. Persecution deepened the sense of community, but it was always strong, even when free of persecution in New World refuges. Community centered on Sunday meetings. These were largely unplanned, with spontaneous testimony from participants listening intently to the calm, quiet, spiritual voice within, which was then shared with the group.

At first, Quakers were often shunned by the outside world. A cobbler could sell no shoes, a baker no bread. But soon, just the reverse happened. Customers came to see that these merchants were truly honest and reliable—they did not undercharge the rich and overcharge the poor, as others did. If they made a promise or an appointment, they kept it. They were tidy, well organized, frugal, worked hard, and educated their children. Not surprisingly, many became prosperous, even rich, especially after the authorities stopped seizing all their worldly possessions. This was a kind of human laboratory, and possibly one of the sources for Max Weber's ideas on the ethical foundations of capitalism.

There were some other striking features of the Quakers. As serious-minded as they often seemed to others, even puritanical in their avoidance of worldly pleasures and strict Sabbath observance, they nevertheless completely abjured the then prevalent Calvinist doctrine of pre-destination, which held that many, perhaps a majority even of Christians, were damned from birth. Compared to Calvinism, Quakerism was indeed a joyful religion, full of hope and expectations of eternal life, not just for the elect, but for everyone, man, woman, and child. No one held a higher position over anyone else. Paid clergy were forbidden; church leaders and lay people held equal rank. Women were respected as equal in the sight of God. This was a true democracy, and a very radical idea for 17th century England.

George Fox (England 1624–1691) had an absolutely indomitable will, which carried him through beatings, imprisonment, and other severe trials. The story contained in his journal is hard to put down. Even minor Quaker tenets, such as using thee and thou, not removing one's hat as a sign of respect to another, or refusing to swear an oath seemed to generate endless trouble and peril. Remarkably, Fox survived and even had time to visit America and help establish his Church there. As Fox wrote:

> Oh, the blows, punchings, beatings, and
> imprisonments that we underwent for not
> putting off our hats to men! Blessed be

> the Lord, many came to see the vanity of
> that custom of putting off the hat to men,
> and felt the weight of Truth's testimony
> against it.

William Penn, Fox's most famous convert, a wealthy Englishman who founded Pennsylvania in America as a refuge for persecuted Quakers, said of Fox's origins that he

> was brought up in country business; and
> as he took most delight in sheep, so he was
> very skillful in them; an employment that
> very well suited his mind in several respects,
> both for its innocence and solitude. . . .

> In 1652, age 28, he being in his usual retire-
> ment to the Lord upon a very high moun-
> tain, in some of the hither parts of York-
> shire . . . he had a vision of the great work
> of God in the earth, and of the way that
> he was to go forth to begin it.

> He was so meek, contented, modest, easy,
> steady, tender, it was a pleasure to be in his
> company. A most merciful man, he was as
> ready to forgive as unapt to take or give offense.

This steadiness, refusal to strike back, and readiness to forgive would be put to truly biblical tests:

From thence I went into the island of Walney; and after the priest had done I spoke to him, but he got away. Then I declared the truth to the people, but they were something rude. I went to speak with the priest at his house, but he would not be seen. The people said he went to hide himself in the haymow; and they looked for him there, but could not find him. Then they said he was gone to hide himself in the standing corn, but they could not find him there either. I went to James Lancaster's, in the island, who was convinced, and from thence returned to Swarthmore, where the Lord's power seized upon Margaret Fell,* her daughter Sarah, and several others.

Justice Saurey came and took me from the people, led me out of the steeple-house, and put me into the hands of the constables and other officers, bidding them whip me, and put me out of the town. They led me about a quarter of a mile, some taking hold by my collar, some by my arms and shoulders; and they shook and dragged me along.

---

* Fox's future wife.

When they had haled me to the common moss-side, a multitude following, the constables and other officers gave me some blows over my back with their willow rods, and thrust me among the rude multitude, who, having furnished themselves with staves, hedge-stakes, holm or holly bushes, fell upon me, and beat me on my head, arms, and shoulders, till they had deprived me of sense; so that I fell down upon the wet common.

When I recovered again, and saw myself lying in a watery common, and the people standing about me, I lay still a little while, and the power of the Lord sprang through me, and the eternal refreshings revived me; so that I stood up again in the strengthening power of the eternal God, and stretching out my arms toward them, I said, with a loud voice, "Strike again; here are my arms, my head, and my cheeks."

There was in the company a mason, a professor,* but a rude fellow, who with his walking rule-staff gave me a blow with all his might just over the back of my hand, as it was stretched out; with which blow

---

* Fox means a person who professes and teaches the Christian religion.

my hand was so bruised, and my arm so benumbed, that I could not draw it to me again. Some of the people cried, "He hath spoiled his hand for ever having the use of it anymore." But I looked at it in the love of God (for I was in the love of God to all that persecuted me), and after awhile the Lord's power sprang through me again, and through my hand and arm, so that in a moment I recovered strength in my hand and arm in the sight of them all.

After awhile there came a man with a pistol, whereupon the people ran out of doors. He called for me; and when I came out to him he snapped his pistol at me, but it would not go off. This caused the people to make a great bustle about him; and some of them took hold of him, to prevent his doing mischief. But I was moved in the Lord's power to speak to him; and he was so struck by the power of the Lord that he trembled for fear, and went and hid himself. Thus the Lord's power came over them all, though there was a great rage in the country.

Next morning I went over in a boat to James Lancaster's. As soon as I came to land there rushed out about forty men with staves, clubs, and fishing poles, who fell upon me, beating and punching me, and endeavoring to thrust me backward into the sea. When they had thrust me almost into the sea, and I saw they would knock me down in it, I went up into the midst of them; but they laid at me again, and knocked me down, and stunned me.

Now were great threatenings given forth in Cumberland that if ever I came there they would take away my life. When I heard it I was drawn to go into Cumberland; and went to Miles Wennington's, in the same parish from which those threatenings came: but they had not power to touch me.

There I lay till the assizes came, and then all the talk was that I was to be hanged. The high sheriff, Wilfred Lawson, stirred them much up to take away my life, and said he would guard me to my execution himself. They were in a rage, and set three musketeers for guard upon me, one at my chamber door, another at the stairs-foot, and a third at the street door; and they would let none come at me, except one sometimes, to bring me some necessary things.

The next day, after the judges were gone out of town, an order was sent to the jailer to put me down into the prison amongst the . . . thieves, and murderers; which accordingly he did. A filthy, nasty place it was, where men and women were put together in a very uncivil manner, and never a house of office to it; and the prisoners were so lousy that one woman was almost eaten to death with lice. Yet bad as the place was, the prisoners were all made very loving and subject to me, and some of them were convinced of the Truth, as the publicans and harlots were of old; so that they were able to confound any priest that might come to the grates to dispute.

But the jailer was cruel, and the under-jailer very abusive both to me and to Friends that came to see me; for he would beat with a great cudgel Friends who did but come to the window to look in upon me. I could get up to the grate, where sometimes I took in my meat; at which the jailer was often offended. Once he came in a great rage and beat me with his cudgel, though I was not at the grate at that time; and as he beat me, he cried, "Come out of the window," though I was then far from it. While he struck me,

I was moved in the Lord's power to sing, which made him rage the more.

Not long after this the Lord's power came over the justices, and they were made to set me at liberty.

The next prison, the notorious Doomsdale, was even worse:

The place was so noisome that it was observed few that went in did ever come out again in health. There was no latrine ... in it; and the excrement of the prisoners that from time to time had been put there had not been carried out (as we were told) for many years. So that it was all like mire, and in some places to the tops of the shoes in water and urine; and the jailer would not let us cleanse it, nor suffer us to have beds or straw to lie on.

At night some friendly people of the town brought us a candle and a little straw; and we burned a little of our straw to take away the stink. The thieves lay over our heads, and the head jailer in a room by them, over our heads also. It seems the smoke went up into the room where the jailer lay; which put him into such a rage that he took the pots of excrement from the thieves and poured them through a hole upon our heads in Doomsdale, till we were so bespattered that we could not touch ourselves nor one another. And the stink increased upon us; so that what with stink, and what with smoke, we were almost choked and smothered. We had the stink under our feet before, but now we had it on our heads and backs also; and he having quenched our straw with the filth he poured down, had made a great smother in the place. Moreover, he railed at us most hideously, calling us hatchet-faced dogs, and such strange names as we had never heard of. In this manner we were obliged to stand all night, for we could not sit down, the place was so full of filthy excrement.

This jailer was himself eventually put in Doomsdale, where he died, but Fox faced further tortures:

After some further discourse they committed me to prison again, there to lie until the next assize; and colonel Kirby gave order to the jailer to keep me close, "and suffer no flesh alive to come at me," for I was not fit, he said, "to be discoursed with by men." I was put into a tower where the smoke of the other prisoners came up so thick it stood as dew upon the walls, and sometimes it was so thick that I could hardly see the candle when it burned; and I being locked under three locks, the under-jailer, when the smoke was great, would hardly be persuaded to come up to unlock one of the uppermost doors for fear of the smoke, so that I was almost smothered.

Besides, it rained in upon my bed, and many times, when I went to stop out the rain in the cold winter season, my shirt was as wet as muck with the rain that came in upon me while I was laboring to stop it out. And the place being high and open to the wind, sometimes as fast as I stopped it the wind blew it out again. In this manner I lay all that long, cold winter till the next assize, in which time I was so starved, and so frozen with cold and wet with the rain that my body was greatly swelled and my limbs much benumbed.

They then removed me into a worse room, where I had neither chimney nor fire hearth. This being towards the seaside and lying much open, the wind drove in the rain forcibly so that the water came over my bed, and ran so about the room that I was fain to skim it up with a platter. When my clothes were wet, I had no fire to dry them; so that my body was benumbed with cold, and my fingers swelled so that one was grown as big as two.

But though they would not let Friends come to me, they would often bring others, either to gaze upon me, or to contend with me. One time a great company of Papists came to discourse with me. They affirmed that the Pope was infallible, and had stood infallible ever since Peter's time. But I showed them the contrary by history; for one of the bishops of Rome (Marcellinus by name), denied the faith and sacrificed to idols; therefore he was not infallible. I told them that if they were in the infallible Spirit, they need not have jails, swords, and staves, racks and tortures, fires and faggots, whips and gallows, to hold up their religion, and to destroy men's lives about it; for if they were in the infallible Spirit, they would preserve men's lives, and use none but spiritual weapons about religion.

Fox's indefatigable powers of argumentation were also employed against the many judges he met in courtrooms. When asked to swear on a Bible, which the judge knows he will not do, he simply asks for the Bible. When in his hand, he opens it and reads the passage in which Jesus forbids swearing. This was powerful testimony, because the Bible, especially, the word of Jesus, was the highest possible authority in 17th century England. Nor did Fox need the Bible in hand. He had memorized what seemed to be every word of it, and could always pull up from memory the passage or passages needed to refute his accusers and enemies.

Judges also came to be apprehensive of Fox's legal skills. Being at the dock so often, Fox learned quickly and often turned the tables on the court:

> Then the clerk read the indictment, and I told the Judge I had something to speak to it; for I had informed myself of the errors that were in it. . . .

> I asked him whether the oath [which Fox had refused to take] was to be tendered to the King's subjects, or to the subjects of foreign princes. He said, "To the subjects of this realm." "Then," said I, "look into the indictment; ye may see that ye have left out the word 'subject'; so not having named me in the indictment as a subject, ye cannot praemunire [imprison and strip

of possessions] me for not taking an oath."
Then they looked over the statute and the
indictment, and saw it was as I said; and
the Judge confessed it was an error.

In this instance, Fox finds not just one error in
the indictment, but error after error. This legal acu-
men, together with Fox's fearlessness, confidence,
and matchless speaking voice overawed people,
even judges. No wonder that a judge says to him, an
indicted prisoner before the bar: "I will not be afraid
of thee, George Fox."*

It is a gripping story, how an unknown shepherd comes to frighten judges and civil authorities,
through sheer sincerity and indomitable will, and
eventually to establish one of the most influential
religious movements of modern history. As the pre-
ceding excerpts suggest, it is best told in Fox's own
vivid words, as dictated to some trusted companions
toward the end of a remarkable life, and carefully
edited and selected in this edition.

—HUNTER LEWIS

---

* Hunter Lewis ed., *The Essence of George Fox's Journal*, (Mt. Jackson, VA: Axios Press, 2012) 182.

EDITOR'S NOTE

Bracketed matter occuring within the main text of George Fox's *Journal* are notes written by Rufus M. Jones, editor of an earlier edition of the book.

Chapter One
Boyhood—A Seeker
(1624–1648)

W HEN I CAME to 11 years of age, I knew pureness and righteousness; for while a child I was taught how to walk to be kept pure. . . .

As I grew up, my relations thought to have made me a priest of the government-sanctioned and supported Anglican or Presbyterian churches but others persuaded to the contrary. Whereupon I was put to a man who was a shoemaker by trade, and dealt in wool. . . .

Age 19. . . at the command of God, the ninth of the seventh month, 1643, I left my relations, and broke off all familiarity or fellowship with young or old. . . .

Temptations grew more and more, and I was tempted almost to despair; and when Satan could not effect his design upon me that way, he laid snares and baits to draw me to commit some sin, whereof he might take advantage to bring me to despair. . . .

Being returned into Leicestershire, my relations would have had me married; but I told them I was but a lad, and must get wisdom. . . .

I heard . . . of . . . Dr. Cradock, a priest of Coventry, and went to him. I asked him the ground of temptations and despair, and how troubles came to be wrought in man? . . . As we were walking together in his garden, the alley being narrow, I chanced, in turning, to set my foot on the side of a bed, at which the man was in a rage, as if his house had been on fire. Thus all our discourse was lost, and I went away in sorrow, worse than I was when I came. I thought these established priests to be . . . miserable comforters, and saw they were all as nothing to me, for they could not reach my condition.

After this I went to another one, Macham, a priest in high account. He would needs give me some physic, and I was to have . . . let blood; but they could not get one drop of blood from me, either in arms or head (though they endeavored to do so), my body being, as it were, dried up with sorrows, grief and troubles, which were so great upon me that I could have wished I had never been born, or that I had been born blind, that I might never have seen wickedness or vanity; and deaf, that I might never have heard vain and wicked words, or the Lord's name blasphemed. . . .

. . . Another time, as I was walking in a field on a First-day morning, the Lord opened unto me that being bred at Oxford or Cambridge was not enough to fit and qualify men to be ministers of Christ; and I wondered at it, because it was the common belief of people. . . .

But the Lord showed me clearly that He did not dwell in these temples which men had commanded and set up, but in people's hearts; for both Stephen and the apostle Paul bore testimony that He did not dwell in temples made with hands, not even in that which He had once commanded to be built, since He put an end to it; but that His people were His temple, and He dwelt in them. . . .

After this I met with a sort of people that held women have no souls, (adding in a light manner), "No more than a goose." But I reproved them, and told them, that was not right; for Mary said, "My soul doth magnify the Lord, and my spirit hath rejoiced in God my Savior. . . ."

I fasted much, walked abroad in solitary places many days, and often took my Bible, and sat in hollow trees and lonesome places till night came on; and frequently in the night walked mournfully about by myself; for I was a man of sorrows in the time of the first workings of the Lord in me.

During all this time I was never joined in profession of Religion with any, but gave up myself to the

Lord, having forsaken all evil company, taken leave of father and mother, and all other relations, and traveled up and down as a stranger in the earth, which way the Lord inclined my heart; taking a chamber to myself in the town where I came, and tarrying, sometimes more, sometimes less, in a place. . . .*

Though my exercises and troubles were very great, yet were they not so continual but that I had some intermissions, and I was sometimes brought into such a heavenly joy that I thought I had been in Abraham's bosom. . . .

. . . After I had received that opening from the Lord, that to be bred at Oxford or Cambridge was not sufficient to fit a man to be a minister of Christ, I regarded the established priests less, and looked more . . . to the Dissenting people.[†] Among them I saw there was some tenderness;[‡] and many of them came afterwards to be convinced [of Fox's teaching]. . . .

But as I had forsaken the priests, so I left the . . . other preachers also . . . ; for I saw there was none among them all that could speak to my condition. . . .

---

* Fox does not say where his money came from. It is possible that he saved enough from early work to cover the expenses of his initial wandering and ministry. Later there were presumably donations from wealthy people such as William Penn.

† Dissenters were members of seats and congregations not sanctioned by the state, especially Congregationalists and Baptists.

‡ Fox often referred to tender people, by which he meant sincere and conscientious people who were open to his teaching.

One day, when I had been walking solitarily abroad, and was come home, I was taken up in the love of God, so that I could not but admire the greatness of His love; and while l was in that condition, it was opened unto me by the eternal light and power, and I therein clearly saw that all was done and to be done in and by Christ, and how He conquers and destroys this tempter the devil, and all his works, and is atop of him; and that all these troubles were good for me, and temptations for the trial of my faith, which Christ had given me.

The Lord opened me, that I saw all through these troubles and temptations. My living faith was raised, that I saw all was done by Christ the life, and my belief was in Him. . . .

I saw, also, that there was an ocean of darkness and death; but an infinite ocean of light and love, which flowed over the ocean of darkness. In that also I saw the infinite love of God, and I had great openings.*

Then came people from far and near to see me; but I was fearful of being drawn out by them; yet I was made to speak, and open things to them. . . .

Then could I say I had been in spiritual Babylon, Sodom, Egypt, and the grave; but by the eternal power of God I was come out of it, and was brought over it, and the power of it, into the power of Christ. . . .

---

* He means "insights."

A report went abroad of me, that I was a young man that had a discerning spirit; whereupon many came to me, from far and near. . . . The Lord's power broke forth, and I had great openings and prophecies, and spoke unto them of the things of God, which they heard with attention and silence, and went away and spread the fame thereof. . . .

Chapter Two

The First Years of Ministry
(1648–1649)

I N 1648 . . . I went to Mansfield, where was a great meeting of professors* and people. Here I was moved to pray; and the Lord's power was so great that the house seemed to be shaken. . . . Passing thence, I met with a great company of professors in Warwickshire, who were praying and expounding the Scriptures in the fields. Upon which they fell into a fierce contention. . . .

After some time I met with some people who had a notion that there was no God, but that all things come by nature. I had a great dispute with them, and

---

* Educated Christian teachers, many of whom were priests.

overturned them, and made some of them confess that there is a living God. . . .

At a certain time, when I was at Mansfield, there was a sitting of the justices about hiring of servants; and it was upon me from the Lord to go and speak to the justices, that they should not oppress the servants in their wages. . . .

. . . When I was come to the house where they were, and many servants with them, I exhorted the justices not to oppress the servants in their wages, but to do that which was right and just to them; and I exhorted the servants to do their duties, and serve honestly. . . .

. . . I was then moved to go and speak to one of the most wicked men in the country, one who was a common drunkard, a noted whore-master, and a rhyme-maker; and I reproved him in the dread of the mighty God, for his evil courses. . . . This man was convinced, and turned from his wickedness, and remained an honest, sober man, to the astonishment of the people who had known him before.

Thus the work of the Lord went forward, and many were turned from the darkness to the light, within the compass of these three years, 1646, 1647, and 1648. . . .

. . . As the Lord opened these things unto me I felt that His power went forth over all, by which all might be reformed if they would receive and bow unto it. The priests might be reformed and brought into the true faith, which is the gift of God. The lawyers might

be reformed and brought into the law of God. . . .
This lets man see that if he wrongs his neighbor, he
wrongs himself; and teaches him to do unto others
as he would they should do unto him. The physicians
might be reformed and brought into the wisdom of
God, by which all things were made and created; that
they might receive a right knowledge of the creatures,
and understand their virtues, which the Word of wisdom, by which they were made and are upheld, hath
given them. . . .

Now the Lord God opened to me by His invisible
power that every man was enlightened by the divine
Light of Christ, and I saw it shine through all. . . .*

I was sent to turn people from darkness to the
Light, that they might receive Christ Jesus; for to as
many as should receive Him in His Light, I saw He
would give power to become the sons of God; which
power I had obtained by receiving Christ. I was to
direct people to the Spirit that gave forth the Scriptures, by which they might be led into all truth, and
up to Christ and God, as those had been who gave
them forth.

Yet I had no slight esteem of the Holy Scriptures.
They were very precious to me; for I was in that Spirit
by which they were given forth; and what the Lord

---

* This is a central tenet of Fox's teaching. Each of us has an inner voice,
given us by God, which, if listened to, will direct us throughout our lives.

opened in me I afterwards found was agreeable to them. I could speak much of these things, and many volumes might be written upon them. . . .

. . . It was given to me, as I traveled up and down, I was not to bid people Good morrow, or Good evening; neither might I bow or scrape with my leg to any one; and this made . . . people rage. Oh, the blows, punchings, beatings, and imprisonments that we underwent for not putting off our hats to men! . . . Blessed be the Lord, many came to see the vanity of that custom of putting off the hat to men, and felt the weight of Truth's testimony against it.

About this time I was sorely exercised in going to their courts to cry for justice, in speaking and writing to judges and justices to do justly; in warning such as kept public houses for entertainment that they should not let people have more drink than would do them good; in testifying against wakes, feasts, May-games, sports, plays, and shows, which trained up people to vanity and looseness, and led them from the fear of God. . . .

In fairs, also, and in markets, I was made to declare against their deceitful merchandise, cheating, and cozening; warning all to deal justly, to speak the truth, to let their yea be yea, and their nay be nay, and to do unto others as they would have others do unto them; forewarning them of the great and terrible day of the Lord, which would come upon them all.

I was moved, also, to cry against all sorts of music, and against the mountebanks playing tricks on their stages. . . .

. . . Oh, the vast sums of money that are gotten by the trade they make of selling the Scriptures, and by their preaching, from the highest bishop to the lowest priest! What one trade . . . in the world is comparable to it? Notwithstanding the Scriptures were given forth freely, and Christ commanded His ministers to preach freely, and the prophets and apostles denounced judgment against all covetous hirelings and diviners for money. . . .

Chapter Three

The Challenge and the First Taste of Prison

(1648–1649)

THE LORD SAID unto me, "Thou must go cry against yonder great idol, and against the worshippers therein. . . ."* The Lord's power was so mighty upon me, and so strong in me, that I could not hold, but was made to cry out and say, "Oh, no; it is not the Scriptures taught here!" . . .

As I spoke thus amongst them, the officers came and took me away, and put me into a nasty, stinking

---

* Fox interrupts a sermon of an established priest, which is illegal. Rejoinder was allowed, but not during the sermon. This instance was an exception; Fox generally waited until the other preacher had finished.

prison; the smell whereof got so into my nose and throat that it very much annoyed me. . . .

. . . After some discourse between them and me, they sent me back to prison again. . . . This time, I lodged at the sheriff's, and great meetings we had in his house. Some persons of considerable condition in the world came to them, and the Lord's power appeared eminently amongst them. . . .

The Lord's power was with this friendly sheriff, and wrought a mighty change in him; and great openings he had.

The next market day, as he was walking with me in the chamber, he said, "I must go into the market, and preach repentance to the people." Accordingly he went in his slippers into the market, and into several streets, and preached repentance to the people. Several others also in the town were moved to speak to the mayor and magistrates, and to the people, exhorting them to repent. Hereupon the magistrates grew very angry, sent for me from the sheriff's house, and committed me to the common prison. . . .

After I was set at liberty from Nottingham jail, where I had been kept prisoner a pretty long time, I traveled as before, in the work of the Lord. . . .

Many great and wonderful things were wrought by the heavenly power in those days; for the Lord made bare His omnipotent arm, and manifested His power, to the astonishment of many, by the healing virtue whereby many have been delivered from great infirmities. . . .

. . . While I was at Mansfield-Woodhouse, I was moved to go to the steeple-house established church there, and declare the truth to the priest and people; but the people fell upon me in great rage, struck me down, and almost stifled and smothered me; and I was cruelly beaten and bruised by them with their hands, and with Bibles and sticks. Then they . . . pulled me up, though I was hardly able to stand, and put me into the stocks, where I sat some hours; and they brought dog whips and horse whips, threatening to whip me.

After some time they had me before the magistrate, . . . a knight's house, where were many great persons; who, seeing how evilly I had been used, after much threatening, set me at liberty. But the rude people stoned me out of the town, for preaching the Word of life to them. . . .

Passing thence, I heard of a people in prison at Coventry for religion. As I walked towards the jail, the word of the Lord came to me, saying, "My love was always to thee, and thou art in my love. . . ."

Then, speaking to the people in jail who . . . said that they were God, I asked them if they knew whether it would rain tomorrow. They said they could not tell. I told them God could tell. I asked them if they thought they should be always in that condition, or should change. They answered that they could not tell. "Then," said I, "God can tell, and He doth not change. You say you are God, and yet you cannot tell whether you shall change or no." So they were confounded, and quite brought down for the time.

After I had reproved them for their blasphemous expressions, I went away; for I perceived they were Ranters. . . . Not long after this one of these Ranters, whose name was Joseph Salmon, published a recantation; upon which they were set at liberty.

Chapter Four

A Year in Derby Jail
(1650–1651)

THERE WAS IN a . . . town a great man that had long lain sick, and was given up by the physicians; and some Friends in the town desired me to go to see him. I went up to him in his chamber, and spoke the Word of life to him, and was moved to pray by him; and the Lord was entreated, and restored him to health. . . .

But they had me before the mayor, and threatened to send me, with some others, to the house of correction, and kept us in custody till it was late in the night. Then the officers, with the watchmen, put us out of the town, leaving us to shift as we could. So I bent my course towards Derby, having a friend or two with me. In our way we met with many professors; and at Kidsey Park many were convinced.

. . . At Derby, a woman . . . said there was to be a great lecture . . . that day, and many of the officers of the army, and priests, and preachers were to be there, and a colonel, that was a preacher. Then was I moved of the Lord to go up to them; and when they had done I spoke to them what the Lord commanded me, and they were pretty quiet. But there came an officer and took me by the hand, and said that I and the other two that were with me must go before the magistrates. It was about the first hour after noon that we came before them.

They asked me why we came thither. I said God moved us so to do; and I told them, "God dwells not in temples made with hands." I told them also that all their preaching, baptism, and sacrifices would never sanctify them, and bade them look unto Christ within them, and not unto men; for it is Christ that sanctifies. Then they ran into many words; but I told them they were not to dispute of God and Christ, but to obey Him.

The power of God thundered among them, and they did fly like chaff before it. They put me in and out of the room often, hurrying me backward and forward, for they were from the first hour till the ninth at night in examining me. Sometimes they would tell me in a deriding manner that I was taken up in raptures.

At last they asked me whether I was sanctified. I answered, "Yes; for I am in the paradise of God." Then they asked me if I had no sin. I answered, "Christ my Savior has taken away my sin; and in Him there is no sin." They asked how we knew that Christ did abide in us. I said, "By His Spirit, that He hath given us." They temptingly asked if any of us were Christ. I answered, "Nay; we are nothing; Christ is all." They said, "If a man steal, is it no sin?" I answered, "All unrighteousness is sin."

When they had wearied themselves in examining me, they committed me and one other man to the house of correction in Derby for six months, as blasphemers. . . .*

The keeper of the prison, being a high professor, was greatly enraged against me, and spoke very wickedly of me; but it pleased the Lord one day to strike him, so that he was in great trouble and under much terror of mind. And, as I was walking in my chamber I heard a doleful noise, and, standing still, I heard him say to his wife, "Wife, I have seen the day of judgment, and I saw George there; and I was afraid of him, because I had done him so much wrong, and spoken so much against him to the ministers and professors, and to the justices, and in taverns and alehouses. . . ."

---

* An act of 1648 had made blasphemy, defined as denial of Orthodox, Creedal Christianity, punishable by imprisonment or death.

When the morning came he rose and went to the justices, and told them that he and his house had been plagued for my sake. One of the justices replied (as he reported to me) that the plagues were upon them, too, for keeping me. This was Justice Bennet, of Derby, who was the first that called us Quakers, because I bade them tremble at the word of the Lord. This was in the year 1650. . . .

So I was taken up before the justices; and because I would not consent that they or any should be bound for me* (for I was innocent of any ill behavior, and had spoken the Word of life and truth unto them), Justice Bennet rose up in a rage; and, as I was kneeling down to pray to the Lord to forgive him, he ran upon me, and struck me with both his hands, crying, "Away with him, jailer; take him away, jailer." Whereupon I was taken again to prison, and there kept till the time of my commitment for six months was expired.

But I had now the liberty of leaving prison and walking a mile by myself, which I made use of as I felt freedom. Sometimes I went into the market and streets, and warned the people to repent of their wickedness, and returned to prison again. . . .

. . . The keeper of the house of correction was then commanded to bring me before the commissioners

---

* Put up bail.

and soldiers in the marketplace, where they offered me that preferment, as they called it, asking me if I would not take up arms for the Commonwealth against Charles Stuart.* I told them I knew whence all wars arose, even from the lusts, . . . and that I lived in the virtue of that life and power that took away the occasion of all wars. . . . [†]

Then their rage got up, and they said, "Take him away, jailer, and put him into the prison amongst the rogues and felons." So I was put into a lousy, stinking place, without any bed, amongst thirty felons, where I was kept almost half a year; [‡] yet at times they would let me walk to the garden, believing I would not go away. . . .

The time of Worcester fight coming on, Justice Bennet sent constables to press me to become . . . a soldier, seeing I would not voluntarily accept . . . a command. I told them that I was brought off from outward wars. . . . Being disappointed, they were angry, and committed me close prisoner, without bail. . . . At length they were made to turn me out of jail, about the beginning of winter, in the year 1651, after I had been a prisoner in Derby almost a year—

---

* This is during the English Civil War that ultimately led to the overthrow and execution of Charles I. Fox is offered release if he will become an officer in Oliver Cromwell's army fighting against the King.

† The first mention of Fox's famous doctrine of pacifism. See Benjamin Franklin's *Autobiography* for how later Quakers in America found a way of evading the spirit of the doctrine while observing its letter.

‡ An additional half a year.

six months in the house of correction, and the rest of the time in the common jail.

Chapter Five

One Man May Shake the Country for Ten Miles
(1651–1652)

I WAS COMMANDED BY the Lord to pull off my shoes. I stood still, for it was winter; and the Word of the Lord was like a fire in me. So I put off my shoes, and left them with the shepherds; and the poor shepherds trembled and were astonished. Then I walked on about a mile, and as soon as I was got within the city, the Word of the Lord came to me again, saying, "Cry, Woe to the bloody city of Lichfield! . . ."

As I went thus crying through the streets, there seemed to me to be a channel of blood running down the streets, and the marketplace appeared like a pool of blood.

When I had declared what was upon me, and felt myself clear, I went out of the town in peace, and, returning to the shepherds, I gave them some money, and took my shoes of them again. But the fire of the Lord was so in my feet, and all over me, that I did not matter to put on my shoes again, and was at a stand whether I should or no, till I felt freedom from the Lord so to do; then, after I had washed my feet, I put on my shoes again.

After this a deep consideration came upon me, for what reason I should be sent to cry against that city, and call it the bloody city! . . . But afterwards I came to understand, that in the Emperor Diocletian's time a thousand Christians were martyred in Lichfield.

Passing on, I was moved of the Lord to go to Beverley steeple-house, which was then a place of high profession; and being very wet with rain, I went first to an inn. As soon as I came to the door, a young woman of the house came to the door, and said, "What, is it you? Come in," as if she had known me before; for the Lord's power bowed their hearts. So I refreshed myself and went to bed; and in the morning, my clothes being still wet, I got ready, and having paid for what I had in the inn, I went up to the steeple-house, where was a man preaching. When he had done, I was moved to speak to him, and to the people, in the mighty power of God, and to turn them to their teacher, Christ Jesus. The power of the Lord was so strong, that it struck a mighty dread amongst the people. The mayor came and spoke a few words to me; but none of them had any power to meddle with me. . . .

I went to another steeple-house about three miles off, where preached a great high priest, called a doctor . . . I went in . . . and stayed till the priest had done. The words which he took for his text were these, ". . . Every one that thirsteth, come ye to the waters; and he that hath no money, come ye, buy and eat, yea come, buy wine and milk without money and without price."

Then was I moved of the Lord God to say unto him, "Come down, thou deceiver; dost thou bid people come freely, and take of the water of life freely, and yet thou takest three hundred pounds a year of them for preaching the Scriptures to them.* Mayest thou not blush for shame? Did the prophet Isaiah, and Christ do so, who spoke the words, and gave them forth freely? Did not Christ say to His ministers, whom He sent to preach, 'freely ye have received, freely give'?"

The priest, like a man amazed, hastened away. After he had left his flock, I had as much time as I could desire to speak to the people; and I directed them from the darkness to the Light, and to the grace of

---

* As a priest of the official church, he was salaried. Three hundred pounds a year was a large living.

God that would teach them, and bring them salvation; to the Spirit of God in their inward parts, which would be a free teacher unto them. . . .

Thence I passed on through the country, and came at night to an inn where was a company of rude people. I bade the woman of the house, if she had any meat, to bring me some; but because I said Thee and Thou* to her, she looked strangely on me. I asked her if she had any milk. She said, No. I was sensible she spake falsely; and, being willing to try her further, I asked her if she had any cream? She denied that she had any.

There stood a churn in the room, and a little boy, playing about, put his hands into it and pulled it down, and threw all the cream on the floor before my eyes. Thus was the woman manifested to be a liar. She was amazed, blessed herself, took up the child, and whipped it sorely: but I reproved her for her lying and deceit. After the Lord had thus discovered her deceit and perverseness, I walked out of the house, and went away till I came to a stack of hay, and lay in the haystack that night, in rain and snow, it being but three days before the time called Christmas.

The next day I came into York, where were several very tender people. Upon the First-day following, I

---

* Quakers were celebrated for using thee and thou instead of you. This was the familiar rather than formal second person form. Eventually thee and thou disappeared entirely from vernacular English, although it could still be found in the King James translation of the Bible.

was commanded of the Lord to go and speak to priest Bowles and his hearers in their great cathedral. Accordingly I went. When the priest had done, I told them I had something from the Lord God to speak to the priest and people. "Then say on quickly," said a professor, for there was frost and snow, and it was very cold weather. Then I told them that this was the Word of the Lord God unto them—that they lived in words, but God Almighty looked for fruits amongst them.

As soon as the words were out of my mouth, they hurried me out, and threw me down the steps. But I got up again without hurt, and went to my lodging, and several were convinced there. . . .

Another priest sent word to have a dispute with me, and Friends went with me to the house where he was; but when he understood we were come, he slipped out of the house, and hid himself under a hedge. The people went and found him, but could not get him to come to us. . . .

In this way, I was sent of the Lord God of heaven and earth to preach freely, and to bring people off from these outward temples made with hands, which God dwelleth not in; that they might know their bodies to become the temples of God and of Christ; and to draw people off from all their superstitious ceremonies, Jewish and heathenish customs, traditions, and doctrines of men; and from all the world's hireling teachers, that take tithes and great wages, preaching for hire, and divining for money, whom God and Christ never sent, as themselves confess when they say that they never heard God's nor Christ's voice. I exhorted the people to come off from all these things, directing them to the Spirit and grace of God in themselves, and to the Light of Jesus in their own hearts; that they might come to know Christ, their free teacher, to bring them salvation, and to open the Scriptures to them. . . .

Next . . . I came towards Cranswick, to Captain Pursloe's and Justice Hotham's, who received me kindly, being glad that the Lord's power had so appeared; that truth was spread, and so many had received it. Justice Hotham said that if God had not raised up this principle of Light and life which I preached, the nation would have been overrun with Ranterism,* and all the justices in the nation could not have stopped it with all their laws. . . .

When I had cleared myself I went to an inn, and desired them to let me have a lodging; but they would not. I desired a little meat or milk, and said I would pay for it; but they refused. So I walked out of the town, and a company of fellows followed, and asked me, "What news?" I bade them repent, and fear the Lord.

---

* Ranters, unlike Quakers, differed from orthodox Christian doctrine, and also among themselves. Some were accused of loose sexual behavior. The Act of 1648, demanding religious conformity, was intended to catch Ranters but often led to trouble for the Quakers.

After I was gone a pretty way, I came to another house, and desired the people to let me have a little meat, drink, and lodging for my money; but they denied me. I went to another house, and desired the same; but they refused me also. By this time it was grown so dark that I could not see the highway; but I discerned a ditch, and got a little water, and refreshed myself. Then I got over the ditch; and, being weary with traveling, I sat down amongst the furze bushes till it was day.

About break of day I got up, and passed on over the fields. A man came after me with a great pikestaff and went along with me to a town; . . . he raised the town upon me, with the constable and chief constable, before the sun was up. I declared God's everlasting truth amongst them, warning them of the day of the Lord, that was coming upon all sin and wickedness; and exhorted them to repent. But they seized me, and had me back to Patrington, about three miles, guarding me with watch-bills, pikes, staves, and halberds.

When I was come to Patrington, all the town was in an uproar, and the priest and constables were consulting together; so I had another opportunity to declare the Word of life amongst them, and warn them to repent. At last a professor, a tender man, called me into his house, and there I took a little milk and bread, having not eaten for some days before. Then they guarded me about nine miles to a justice. . . .

When I was brought in before him, because I did not put off my hat,* and because I said Thou to him, he asked the man that rode thither before me whether I was not dimwitted. The man told him, No; it was my principle.

I warned him to repent, and come to the Light with which Christ had enlightened him; that by it he might see all his evil words and actions, and turn to Christ Jesus whilst he had time; and that whilst he had time he should prize it. "Ay, ay," said he, "the Light that is spoken of in the third of John." I desired he would mind it, and obey it.

As I admonished him, I laid my hand upon him, and he was brought down by the power of the Lord; and all the watchmen stood amazed. Then he took me into a little parlor with the other man, and desired to see what I had in my pockets of letters or intelligence. I plucked out my linen, and showed him I had no letters. He said, "He is not a vagrant, by his linen"; then he set me at liberty. . . .

Then I returned to Patrington again, and visited those Friends that were convinced there; by whom I understood that a tailor, and some wild blades in that town, had occasioned my being carried before the justice. The tailor came to ask my forgiveness,

---

* Fox and other Quakers refused to remove their hats for other men outside a church, however high the other men's office. Since this included officials and judges, it led to endless trouble.

fearing I would complain of him. The constables also were afraid, lest I should trouble them. But I forgave them all, and warned them to turn to the Lord, and to amend their lives.

Now that which made them the more afraid was this: when I was in the steeple-house* at Oram, not long before, there came a professor, who gave me a push on the breast in the steeple-house, and bade me get out of the church. . . . It happened that Justice Hotham came to hear of this man's abuse, sent his warrant for him, and bound him over to the sessions; so affected was he with the Truth and so zealous to keep the peace. And indeed this Justice Hotham had asked me before whether any people had meddled with me, or abused me; but I was not at liberty to tell him anything of that kind, but was to forgive all.

The next First-day I went to Tickhill, whither the Friends of that side gathered together, and a mighty brokenness by the power of God there was amongst the people. I went out of the meeting, being moved of God to go to the steeple-house. When I came there, I found the priest and most of the chief of the parish together in the chancel.

I went up to them, and began to speak; but they immediately fell upon me; the clerk up with his Bible,

---

* Church.

as I was speaking, and struck me on the face with it, so that my face gushed out with blood; and I bled exceedingly in the steeple-house. The people cried, "Let us have him out of the church." When they had got me out, they beat me exceedingly, threw me down, and turned me over a hedge. They afterwards dragged me through a house into the street, stoning and beating me as they dragged me along; so that I was all over besmeared with blood and dirt. They got my hat from me, which I never had again. Yet when I was got upon my legs, I declared the Word of life, showed them the fruits of their teacher, and how they dishonored Christianity. . . .

. . . Friends were much abused that day by the priest and his people: insomuch that some moderate justices hearing of it, two or three of them came and sat at the town to examine the business. He that had shed my blood was afraid of having his hand cut off for striking me in the church, as they called it; but I forgave him, and would not appear against him. . . .

Chapter Six

A New Era Begins
(1652)

THE NEXT DAY we traveled on, and at night got a little fern or bracken to put under us, and lay upon a common. Next morning we reached a town. . . .

. . . In my way I came to a great house, where was a schoolmaster; and they got me into the house. I asked them questions about their religion and worship; and afterwards I declared the truth to them. They had me into a parlor, and locked me in, pretending that I was a young man that was mad, and had run away from my relations; and that they would keep me till they could send to them. But I soon convinced them of their mistake, and they let me forth, and would have had me to stay; but I was not to stay there.

Then having exhorted them to repentance, and directed them to the Light of Christ Jesus, that through it they might come unto Him and be saved, I passed from them, and came in the night to a little alehouse on a common, where there was a company of rude fellows drinking. Because I would not drink with them, they struck me with their clubs; but I reproved them, and brought them to be somewhat cooler; and then I walked out of the house upon the common in the night.

After some time one of these drunken fellows came out, and would have come close up to me, pretending to whisper to me; but I perceived he had a knife; and therefore I kept off him, and bade him repent, and fear God. So the Lord by His power preserved me from this wicked man; and he went into the house again. The next morning I went on through other Dales, warning and exhorting people everywhere as I passed, to repent and turn to the Lord: and several were convinced. At one house that I came to, the man of the house . . . would have given me money, but I would not receive it. . . .*

The next First-day I came to Firbank chapel in Westmoreland, where Francis Howgill and John Audland [followers of Fox] had been preaching in the morning. . . .

---

* Perhaps Fox only accepted money from trusted converts.

While others were gone to dinner, I went to a brook, got a little water, and then came and sat down on the top of a rock hard by the chapel. In the afternoon the people gathered about me, with several of their preachers. It was judged there were above a thousand people; to whom I declared God's everlasting truth and Word of life freely and largely for about the space of three hours. . . .

At . . . Underbarrow . . . as I walked upon a bank . . . there came several poor travelers, asking relief, who I saw were in necessity; and they gave them nothing, but said they were cheats. It grieved me to see such hard-heartedness amongst professors; whereupon, when they were gone in to their breakfast, I ran after the poor people about a quarter of a mile, and gave them some money. . . .

From thence I went into the island of Walney; and after the priest had done I spoke to him, but he got away. Then I declared the truth to the people, but they were something rude. I went to speak with the priest at his house, but he would not be seen. The people said he went to hide himself in the haymow; and they looked for him there, but could not find him. Then they said he was gone to hide himself in the standing corn, but they could not find him there either. I went to James Lancaster's, in the island, who was convinced, and from thence returned to Swarthmore, where the Lord's power seized upon Margaret Fell, her daughter Sarah, and several others. . . .

. . . I found the priests and professors, and that envious Justice Sawrey, had much incensed Judge Fell and Captain Sands against the truth by their lies; but when I came to speak with him I answered all his objections, and so thoroughly satisfied him by the Scriptures that he was convinced in his judgment. . . .

There came to Judge Fell's Captain Sands, before mentioned, endeavoring to incense the Judge against me, for he was an evil-minded man, and full of envy against me; and yet he could speak high things, and use the Scripture words, and say, "Behold, I make all things new." But I told him then he must have a new God, for his God was his belly. Besides him came also that envious justice, John Sawrey. I told him his heart was rotten, and he was full of hypocrisy to the brim. Several other people also came, of whose states the Lord gave me a discerning; and I spoke to their conditions about what they were. . . . A great meeting of Friends was settled there in the Lord's power, which continued near forty years, until the year 1690, when a new meetinghouse was erected near it. . . .*

In the afternoon I went to the steeple-house at Lancaster, and declared the truth to the priest and people, laying open before them the deceit they lived in, and directing them to the power and Spirit of God which

---

* Judge Fell never joined the Friends, but his wife Margaret did, and became a powerful and influential supporter, as we shall see.

they wanted. But they haled me out, and stoned me along the street till I came to John Lawson's house. . . .

After this I returned into Westmoreland, and spoke through Kendal on a market day. So dreadful was the power of God upon me, that people flew like chaff before me into their houses. . . . Several were convinced. . . .

Now began the priests to rage more and more, and as much as they could to stir up persecution. Leading supporters, James Nayler and Francis Howgill, were cast into prison in Appleby jail, at the instigation of the malicious priests, some of whom prophesied that within a month we should be all scattered again, and come to nothing. . . .

On a lecture day I was moved to go to the steeple-house at Ulverstone, where were abundance of professors, priests, and people. . . . The people were quiet, and heard me gladly, till . . . Justice Sawrey (who was the first stirrer-up of cruel persecution in the north) incensed them against me, and set them on to hale, beat, and bruise me. But now on a sudden the people were in a rage, and fell upon me in the steeple-house before his face, knocked me down, kicked me, and trampled upon me. So great was the uproar, that some tumbled over their seats for fear.

At last Sawrey came and took me from the people, led me out of the steeple-house, and put me into the hands of the constables and other officers, bidding them whip me, and put me out of the town. They led me about a quarter of a mile, some taking hold by my collar, some by my arms and shoulders; and they shook and dragged me along.

Many friendly people being come to the market, and some to the steeple-house to hear me, diverse of these they knocked down also, and broke their heads so that the blood ran down from several; and Judge Fell's son running after to see what they would do with me, they threw him into a ditch of water, some of them crying, "Knock the teeth out of his head."

When they had haled me to the common moss-side, a multitude following, the constables and other officers gave me some blows over my back with their willow rods, and thrust me among the rude multitude, who, having furnished themselves with staves, hedge-stakes, holm or holly bushes, fell upon me, and beat me on my head, arms, and shoulders, till they had deprived me of sense; so that I fell down upon the wet common.

When I recovered again, and saw myself lying in a watery common, and the people standing about me, I lay still a little while, and the power of the Lord sprang through me, and the eternal refreshings revived me; so that I stood up again in the strengthening power of the eternal God, and stretching out my arms toward them, I said, with a loud voice, "Strike again; here are my arms, my head, and my cheeks."

There was in the company a mason, a professor, but a rude fellow, who with his walking rule-staff gave me a blow with all his might just over the back of my hand, as it was stretched out; with which blow my hand was so bruised, and my arm so benumbed, that I could not draw it to me again. Some of the people cried, "He hath spoiled his hand for ever having the use of it anymore." But I looked at it in the love of God (for I was in the love of God to all that persecuted me), and after awhile the Lord's power sprang through me again, and through my hand and arm, so that in a moment I recovered strength in my hand and arm in the sight of them all.

Then they began to fall out among themselves. Some of them came to me, and said that if I would give them money they would secure me from the rest. But I was moved of the Lord to declare the Word of life, and showed them their false Christianity, and the fruits of their priest's ministry, telling them that they were more like heathens and Jews than true Christians.

Then was I moved of the Lord to come up again through the midst of the people, and go into Ulverstone market. As I went, there met me a soldier, with his sword by his side. "Sir," said he to me, "I see you are a man, and I am ashamed and grieved that you should be thus abused"; and he offered to assist me in what he could. I told him that the Lord's power was over all;

and I walked through the people in the market, none of whom had power to touch me then. But some of the market people abusing some Friends in the market, I turned about, and saw this soldier among them with his naked rapier; whereupon I ran, and, catching hold of the hand his rapier was in, bid him put up his sword again if he would go along with me.

About two weeks after this I went into Walney Island, and James Nayler went with me. We stayed one night at a little town on this side, called Cockan, and had a meeting there, where one was convinced.

After awhile there came a man with a pistol, whereupon the people ran out of doors. He called for me; and when I came out to him he snapped his pistol at me, but it would not go off. This caused the people to make a great bustle about him; and some of them took hold of him, to prevent his doing mischief. But I was moved in the Lord's power to speak to him; and he was so struck by the power of the Lord that he trembled for fear, and went and hid himself. Thus the Lord's power came over them all, though there was a great rage in the country.

Next morning I went over in a boat to James Lancaster's. As soon as I came to land there rushed out about forty men with staves, clubs, and fishing poles, who fell upon me, beating and punching me, and endeavoring to thrust me backward into the sea. When they had thrust me almost into the sea, and I saw they would knock me down in it, I went up into the midst of them; but they laid at me again, and knocked me down, and stunned me.

When I came to myself, I looked up and saw James Lancaster's wife throwing stones at my face, and her husband, James Lancaster, was lying over me, to keep the blows and the stones off me. For the people had persuaded James Lancaster's wife that I had bewitched her husband, and had promised her that if she would let them know when I came thither they would be my death. And having got knowledge of my coming, many of the town rose up in this manner with clubs and staves to kill me; but the Lord's power preserved me, that they could not take away my life.

At length I got up on my feet, but they beat me down again into the boat; which James Lancaster observing, he presently came into it, and set me over the water from them; but while we were on the water within their reach they struck at us with long poles, and threw stones after us. By the time we were come to the other side, we saw them beating James Nayler; for whilst they had been beating me, he walked up into a field, and they never minded him till I was gone; then they fell upon him, and all their cry was, "Kill him, kill him."

When I was come over to the town again, on the other side of the water, the townsmen rose up with pitchforks, flails, and staves, to keep me out of the town, crying, "Kill him, knock him on the head, bring the cart; and carry him away to the churchyard." So after they had abused me, they drove me some distance out of the town, and there left me.

Then James Lancaster went back to look after James Nayler; and I being now left alone, went to a ditch of water, and having washed myself (for they had besmeared my face, hands, and clothes with miry dirt), I walked about three miles to Thomas Hutton's house, where lodged Thomas Lawson, the priest that was convinced.

When I came in I could hardly speak to them, I was so bruised; only I told them where I left James Nayler. So they took each of them a horse, and went and brought him thither that night. The next day Margaret Fell hearing of it, sent a horse for me; but I was so sore with bruises, I was not able to bear the shaking of the horse without much pain.

When I was come to Swarthmore, Justice Sawrey, and one Justice Thompson, of Lancaster, granted a warrant against me; but Judge Fell coming home, it was not served upon me; for he was out of the country all this time that I was thus cruelly abused. When he came home he sent forth warrants into the isle of Walney, to apprehend all those riotous persons; whereupon some of them fled the country.

James Lancaster's wife was afterwards convinced of the truth, and repented of the evils she had done me;

and so did others of those bitter persecutors also; but the judgments of God fell upon some of them, and destruction is come upon many of them since....

Being come to Lancaster, Justice Sawrey and Justice Thompson having granted a warrant to apprehend me, though I was not apprehended by it, yet hearing of it, I appeared at the sessions, where there appeared against me about forty priests. These had chosen one Marshall, priest of Lancaster, to be their orator; and had provided one young priest, and two priests' sons, to bear witness against me, who had sworn beforehand that I had spoken blasphemy....

There were then in court several who had been at that meeting, wherein the witnesses swore I spoke those blasphemous words which the priests accused me of; and these, being men of integrity and reputation in the country, did declare and affirm in court that the oath which the witnesses had taken against me was altogether false; and that no such words as they had sworn against me were spoken by me at that meeting. Indeed, most of the serious men of that side of the country, then at the sessions, had been at that meeting; and had heard me both at that and at other meetings also....

I was moved of the Lord to speak; and as soon as I began, priest Marshall, the orator for the rest of the priests, went his way....

... I had no sooner spoken these words than about half a dozen priests, that stood behind me, burst into a passion. One of them, whose name was Jackus, amongst other things that he spake against the Truth, said that the Spirit and the letter were inseparable. I replied, "Then everyone that hath the letter hath the Spirit; and they might buy the Spirit with the letter of the Scriptures."

This plain discovery of darkness in the priest moved Judge Fell and Colonel West to reprove them openly, and tell them that according to that position they might carry the Spirit in their pockets as they did the Scriptures. Upon this the priests, being confounded and put to silence, rushed out in a rage against the justices, because they could not have their bloody ends upon me. The justices, seeing the witnesses did not agree, and perceiving that they were brought to answer the priests' envy, and finding that all their evidences were not sufficient in law to make good their charge against me, discharged me. . . .

. . . Thus I was cleared in open sessions of those lying accusations which the malicious priests had laid to my charge: and multitudes of people praised God that day, for it was a joyful day to many. Justice Benson, of Westmoreland, was convinced; and Major Ripan, mayor of the town of Lancaster, also.

. . . For the Lord opened many mouths that day to speak His Word to the priests, and several friendly people and professors reproved them in their inns, and in the streets, so that they fell, like an old rotten house:

and the cry was among the people that the Quakers had got the day, and the priests were fallen.

Chapter Seven

In Prison Again

(1653)

A BOUT THIS TIME I was in a fast for about ten days. . . .

After some time I went to a meeting at Arnside, where was Richard Myer, who had been long lame of one of his arms. I was moved of the Lord to say unto him amongst all the people, "Stand up upon thy legs," for he was sitting down. And he stood up, and stretched out his arm that had been lame a long time, and said, "Be it known unto you, all people, that this day I am healed." Yet his parents could hardly believe it; but after the meeting was done, they had him aside, took off his doublet, and then saw it was true.

He came soon after to Swarthmore meeting, and there declared how the Lord had healed him. Yet after this the Lord commanded him to go to York with a message from Him, which he disobeyed; and the Lord struck him again, so that he died about three-quarters of a year after.

Now were great threatenings given forth in Cumberland that if ever I came there they would take away my life. When I heard it I was drawn to go into Cumberland;* and went to Miles Wennington's, in the same parish from which those threatenings came: but they had not power to touch me. . . .

The London priest was preaching. He gathered up all the Scriptures he could think of that spoke of false prophets, and antichrists, and deceivers, and threw them upon us; but when he had done I recollected all those Scriptures,[†] and brought them back upon himself. Then the people fell upon me in a rude manner; but the constable charged them to keep the peace, and so made them quiet again. Then the priest began to rage, and said I must not speak there. I told him he had his hourglass, by which he had preached; and he having done, the time was free for me, as well as for him, for he was but a stranger there himself. . . .

When I came down again to Joseph Nicholson's house, I saw a great hole in my coat, which was cut

---

* This is characteristic of Fox.

†Fox often relies on his almost complete command of scripture to confound his critics.

with a knife; but it was not cut through my doublet, for the Lord had prevented their mischief. . . .

. . . I walked up and down in the fields that night, as very often I used to do, and did not go to bed. . . .

After this I went to a village, and many people accompanied me. As I was sitting in a house full of people, declaring the Word of life unto them, I cast mine eye upon a woman, and discerned an unclean spirit in her. And I was moved of the Lord to speak sharply to her, and told her she was under the influence of an unclean spirit; whereupon she went out of the room. Now, I being a stranger there, and knowing nothing of the woman outwardly, the people wondered at it, and told me afterwards that I had discovered a great thing; for all the country looked upon her to be a wicked person.

. . . There came also at another time another woman, and stood at a distance from me, and I cast mine eye upon her, and said, "Thou hast been a harlot"; for I perfectly saw the condition and life of the woman. The woman answered and said that many could tell her of her outward sins, but none could tell her of her inward. Then I told her her heart was not right before the Lord, and that from the inward came the outward. This woman came afterwards to be convinced of God's truth, and became a Friend.

. . . After the meeting, the pastor of the Baptists, . . . a flashy man, asked me what must be damned. I was moved immediately to tell him that that which spoke in him was to be damned. This stopped his mouth.... He came afterwards to be convinced....

On the market day I went up into the market, to the market cross. The magistrates had both threatened and sent their sergeants; and the magistrates' wives had said that if I came there they would pluck the hair off my head; and the sergeants should take me up. Nevertheless I obeyed the Lord God, went up on the cross, and declared unto them that the day of the Lord was coming upon all their deceitful ways and doings, and deceitful merchandise; that they should put away all cozening and cheating, and keep to Yea and Nay, and speak the truth one to another. So the Truth and the power of God was set over them....

The next day, the justices and magistrates of the town being gathered together in the town hall, they granted a warrant against me, and sent for me before them. I was then gone to a Baptist's; but hearing of it, I went up to the hall, where many rude people were, some of whom had sworn false things against me.... After a large examination they committed me to prison as a blasphemer, a heretic, and a seducer, though they could not justly charge any such thing against me.

The jail at Carlisle had two jailers, an upper and an under, who looked like two great bear-wards. When I was brought in the upper jailer took me up into a great chamber, and told me I should have what I would in that room. But I told him he should not expect any money from me, for I would neither lie in any of his beds, nor eat any of his victuals. Then he put me into another room, where after awhile I got something to lie upon.

There I lay till the assizes came, and then all the talk was that I was to be hanged. The high sheriff, Wilfred Lawson, stirred them much up to take away my life, and said he would guard me to my execution himself. They were in a rage, and set three musketeers for guard upon me, one at my chamber door, another at the stairs-foot, and a third at the street door; and they would let none come at me, except one sometimes, to bring me some necessary things. . . .

The next day, after the judges were gone out of town, an order was sent to the jailer to put me down into the prison amongst the . . . thieves, and murderers; which accordingly he did. A filthy, nasty place it was, where men and women were put together in a very uncivil manner, and never a house of office to it; and the prisoners were so lousy that one woman was almost eaten to death with lice. Yet bad as the place was, the prisoners were all made very loving and subject to me, and some of them were convinced of the Truth, as the publicans and harlots were of old; so that they were able to confound any priest that might come to the grates to dispute.

But the jailer was cruel, and the under-jailer very abusive both to me and to Friends that came to see me; for he would beat with a great cudgel Friends who did but come to the window to look in upon me. I could get up to the grate, where sometimes I took in my meat; at which the jailer was often offended. Once he came in a great rage and beat me with his cudgel, though I was not at the grate at that time; and as he beat me, he cried, "Come out of the window," though I was then far from it. While he struck me, I was moved in the Lord's power to sing, which made him rage the more....

Not long after this the Lord's power came over the justices, and they were made to set me at liberty. But some time previous the governor and Anthony Pearson came down into the dungeon, to see the place where I was kept and understand what usage I had had. They found the place so bad and the savor so ill, that they cried shame on the magistrates for suffering the jailer to do such things. They called for the jailers into the dungeon, and required them to find sureties for their good behavior; and the under-jailer, who had been such a cruel fellow, they put into the dungeon with me....

Now I went into the country, and had mighty great meetings. The everlasting gospel and Word of life flourished, and thousands were turned to the Lord Jesus Christ, and to His teaching....

Some dangers at this time I underwent in my travels. . . . However, they fell upon us, and had like to have spoiled us and our horses;* but the Lord restrained them, that they did not much hurt; and we passed away. . . .

. . . The everlasting Word of life was freely preached, and freely received; and many hundreds were turned to Christ, their teacher. . . .

Then these professors said that the outward body was the body of death and sin. I showed them their mistake in that also; for Adam and Eve had each of them an outward body, before the body of death and sin got into them; and that man and woman will have bodies when the body of sin and death is put off again; when they are renewed again into the image of God by Christ Jesus, in which they were before they fell. So they ceased at that time from opposing further; and glorious meetings we had in the Lord's power. . . .

A great convincement there was in Cumberland, Bishoprick, Northumberland, Westmoreland, Lancashire, and Yorkshire; and the plants of God grew and flourished, the heavenly rain descending, and God's glory shining upon them. Many mouths were opened by the Lord to His praise. . . .

---

* Travel by horse was expensive, but the funds were apparently available.

Chapter Eight

A Visit to Oliver Cromwell
(1653–1654)

AT THE FIRST convincement, when Friends could not put off their hats to people, or say You to a single person, but Thou and Thee—when they could not bow, or use flattering words in salutation, or adopt the fashions and customs of the world, many Friends, that were tradesmen of several sorts, lost their customers at first, for the people were shy of them, and would not trade with them; so that for a time some Friends could hardly get money enough to buy bread.

But afterwards, when people came to have experience of Friends' honesty and faithfulness, and found that their yea was yea, and their nay was nay; that they kept to a word in their dealings, and would not cozen and cheat, but that if a child were sent to their shops for anything, he was as well used as his parents would have been—then the lives and conversation of Friends did preach, and reached to the witness of God in the people.

Then things altered so, that all the inquiry was, "Where is there a draper, or shopkeeper, or tailor, or shoemaker, or any other tradesman, that is a Quaker?" Then the envious professors altered their note,* and began to cry out, "If we let these Quakers alone, they will take the trade of the nation out of our hands. . . ."

About this time . . . an oath . . . to Oliver Cromwell was . . . required of the soldiers, with the result that many Quakers . . . were . . . discharged because, in obedience to Christ, they could not swear. . . . †

Thence I went to Drayton in Leicestershire to visit my relations. As soon as I was come in, Nathaniel Stephens, the priest, having got another priest, and given notice to the country, sent to me to come to them. . . .

The priests would know where tithes were forbidden or ended. I showed them out of the seventh chapter to the Hebrews that not only tithes, but the

---

* They had previously claimed that Quakers would run out of money and become a burden by thronging the public workhouses.

† Quakers never took an oath in God's name or on a Bible, maintaining that Jesus forbade it, which got them in endless legal trouble.

priesthood that took tithes, was ended; and the law by which the priesthood was made, and tithes were commanded to be paid, was ended and annulled. . . .

. . . Before we parted I told them that if the Lord would, I intended to be at the town again that day week. In the interim I went into the country, and had meetings, and came thither again that day week.

Against that time this priest had got seven priests to help him; for priest Stephens had given notice at a lecture on a market day at Adderston, that such a day there would be a meeting and a dispute with me. I knew nothing of it; but had only said I should be in town that day week again. These eight priests had gathered several hundreds of people, even most of the country thereabouts, and they would have had me go into the steeple-house; but I would not go in, but got on a hill, and there spoke to them and the people.

There were with me Thomas Taylor, who had been a priest, James Parnell, and several other Friends. The priests thought that day to trample down Truth; but the Truth overcame them. Then they grew light, and the people rude; and the priests would not stand trial with me; but would be contending here a little and there a little, with one Friend or another. At last one of the priests brought his son to dispute with me; but his mouth was soon stopped. When he could not tell how to answer, he would ask his father; and his father was confounded also, when he came to answer for his son.

So, after they had toiled themselves, they went away in a rage to priest Stephens's house to drink. As they went away, I said, "I never came to a place where so many priests together would not stand the trial with me. . . ."

. . . Then they took me from that place to the steeple-house wall, and set me on something like a stool; and all the priests being come back, stood under with the people.

The priests cried, "Come, to argument, to argument." I said that I denied all their voices, for they were the voices of hirelings and strangers. They cried, "Prove it, prove it." Then I directed them to the tenth of John, where they might see what Christ said of such. He declared that He was the true Shepherd that laid down His life for His sheep, and His sheep heard His voice and followed Him; but the hireling would fly when the wolf came, because he was a hireling. I offered to prove that they were such hirelings. Then the priests plucked me off the stool again; and they themselves got all upon stools under the steeple-house wall.

Then I felt the mighty power of God arise over all, and I told them that if they would but give audience, and hear me quietly, I would show them by the Scriptures why I denied those eight priests, or teachers, that stood before me, and all the hireling teachers of the world whatsoever; and I would give them Scriptures for what I said. Whereupon both priests and people consented. Then I showed them out of the prophets Isaiah, Jeremiah, Ezekiel, Micah, Malachi, and others, that they were in the steps of such as God sent His true prophets to cry against. . . .

At last one of the priests said that they would read the Scriptures I had quoted. I told them I desired them to do so with all my heart. They began to read the twenty-third of Jeremiah, where they saw the marks of the false prophets that he cried against. When they had read a verse or two I said, "Take notice, people"; but the priests said, "Hold thy tongue, George." I bade them read the whole chapter, for it was all against them. Then they stopped, and would read no further.

My father, though a hearer and follower of the priest, was so well satisfied that he struck his cane upon the ground, and said, "Truly, I see that he that will but stand to the truth, it will bear him out. . . ."

Then I went to Leicester; and from Leicester to Whetstone. . . .

At night they had me before Colonel Hacker,* his major, and captains, a great company of them; and a great deal of discourse we had about the priests, and about meetings; for at this time there was a noise of a plot against Oliver Cromwell. Much reasoning I had

---

* The soldier of Oliver Cromwell's army who had overseen the execution of Charles I. Cromwell had only recently become Lord Protector.

with them about the Light of Christ, which enlight-
eneth every man that cometh into the world. . . .

Then Colonel Hacker said I might go home, and
keep at home, and not go abroad to meetings. I told
him I was an innocent man, free from plots, and
denied all such work. His son Needham said, "Father,
this man hath reigned too long; it is time to have him
cut off." I asked him, "For what? What have I done?
Whom have I wronged? I was bred and born in this
country, and who can accuse me of any evil, from
childhood up?" Colonel Hacker asked me again if I
would go home, and stay at home. I told him that if I
should promise him this, it would manifest that I was
guilty of something, to make my home a prison; and if
I went to meetings they would say I broke their order.
Therefore I told them I should go to meetings as the
Lord should order me, and could not submit to their
requirings; but I said we were a peaceable people.

"Well, then," said Colonel Hacker, "I will send you
tomorrow morning by six o'clock to my Lord Protector, Oliver Cromwell, by Captain Drury, one of his
life-guard. . . ."

Afterwards, when Colonel Hacker was imprisoned
in London, a day or two before his execution,* he was
put in mind of what he had done against the innocent;
and he remembered it, and confessed it to Margaret

---

* Following the restoration of the monarchy.

Fell, saying he knew well whom she meant; and he had trouble upon him for it.

Now I was carried up a prisoner by Captain Drury from Leicester; and when we came to Harborough he asked me if I would go home and stay a fortnight? I should have my liberty, he said, if I would not go to, nor keep meetings. I told him I could not promise any such thing. Several times upon the road did he ask and try me after the same manner, and still I gave him the same answers. So he brought me to London, and lodged me at an inn. . . .

. . . Captain Drury then . . . left me . . . and went to give the Protector an account of me. When he came to me again, he told me that the Protector required that I should promise not to take up a carnal sword or weapon against him or the government, as it then was, and that I should write it in what words I saw good, and set my hand to it. I said little in reply to Captain Drury.

The next morning I was moved of the Lord to write a paper to the Protector, Oliver Cromwell; wherein I did, in the presence of the Lord God, declare that I denied the wearing or drawing of a carnal sword, or any other outward weapon, against him or any man; and that I was sent of God to stand a witness against all violence, and against the works of darkness; and to turn people from darkness to light; and to bring them from the causes of war and fighting, to the peaceable gospel. When I had written what the Lord had given me to write, I set my name to it, and gave it to Captain Drury to hand to Oliver Cromwell, which he did.

After some time Captain Drury brought me before the Protector himself at Whitehall. It was in a morning, before he was dressed. . . .*

I spoke much to him of Truth, and much discourse I had with him about religion; wherein he carried himself very moderately. . . .

Many more words I had with him; but people coming in, I drew a little back. As I was turning, he caught me by the hand, and with tears in his eyes said, "Come again to my house; for if thou and I were but an hour of a day together, we should be nearer one to the other"; adding that he wished me no more ill than he did to his own soul. . . .

Then I went out; and when Captain Drury came out after me he told me the Lord Protector had said I was at liberty, and might go whither I would.

Then I was brought into a great hall, where the Protector's gentlemen were to dine. I asked them what they brought me thither for. They said it was by the Protector's order, that I might dine with them. I bid them let the Protector know that I would not eat of his bread, nor drink of his drink. When he heard this he said, "Now I see there is a people risen that I cannot

---

* Before he did official business.

win with gifts or honors, offices or places; but all other sects and people I can." It was told him again that we had forsaken our own possessions; and were not like to look for such things from him. . . .

During the time I was prisoner at Charing-Cross, there came abundance to see me, almost of all sorts, priests, professors, officers of the army, etc. Once a company of officers, being with me, desired me to pray with them. . . .

Among those that came was Colonel Packer, with several of his officers. While they were with me, there came in one Cob, and a great company of Ranters with him. The Ranters began to call for drink and tobacco; but I desired them to forbear it in my room, telling them if they had such a mind to it, they might go into another room. One of them cried, "All is ours"; and another of them said, "All is well." I replied, "How is all well, while thou art so peevish envious, and crabbed?" for I saw he was of a peevish nature. . . .

This Colonel Packer lived at Theobald's, near Waltham, and was made a justice of the peace. He set up a great meeting of the Baptists at Theobald's Park; for he and some other officers had purchased it. They were exceedingly high, and railed against Friends and Truth, and threatened to apprehend me with their warrants if ever I came there.

. . . After I was set at liberty . . . I . . . went into the city of London, where we had great and powerful meetings.

So great were the throngs of people that I could hardly get to and from the meetings for the crowds; and the Truth spread exceedingly. . . .

A great convincement there was in London; some in the Protector's house and family. I went to see him again, but could not get to him; the officers were grown so rude.

Chapter Nine

A Visit to the Southern Counties which Ends in Launceston Jail

(1655–1656)*

IT CAME UPON me about this time from the Lord to write a short paper and send it forth as an exhortation and warning to the Pope, and to all kings and rulers in Europe.

Besides this I was moved to write a letter to the Protector (so called) to warn him of the mighty work the Lord hath to do in the nations, and the shaking

---

* Fox is now about thirty.

of them; and to beware of his own wit, craft, subtlety, and policy, and of seeking any by-ends to himself.

I traveled till I came to Reading, where I found a few that were convinced of the way of the Lord. I stayed till the First-day, and had a meeting in George Lamboll's orchard; and a great part of the town came to it. A glorious meeting it proved; great convincement there was, and the people were mightily satisfied. . . .

After this I passed to London, where I stayed awhile, and had large meetings; then went into Essex, and came to Cogshall, where was a meeting of about two thousand people, as it was judged, which lasted several hours, and a glorious meeting it was. The Word of life was freely declared, and people were turned to the Lord Jesus Christ their Teacher and Savior, the Way, the Truth, and the Life. . . .

As I passed through Colchester, I went to visit James Parnell* in prison; but the jailer would hardly let us come in or stay with him. Very cruel they were to him. The jailer's wife threatened to have his blood; and in that jail they did destroy him. . . .

We came to Yarmouth, where there was a Friend, Thomas Bond, in prison for the Truth of Christ, and there stayed awhile. There we had some service; and some were turned to the Lord in that town.

---

* Another preacher among the Friends.

Thence we rode to another town, about twenty miles off, where were many tender people; and I was moved of the Lord to speak to them, as I sat on my horse, in several places as I passed along. . . .

We bade the hostler have our horses ready by three in the morning; for we intended to ride to Lynn, about three and thirty miles, next morning. But when we were in bed at our inn, about eleven at night, the constable and officers came, with a great rabble of people, into the inn. They said they were come with a hue-and-cry from a justice of the peace that lived near the town, about five miles off, where I had spoken to the people in the streets, as I rode along. They had been told to search for two horsemen, that rode upon gray horses, and in gray clothes; a house having been broken into the Seventh-day before at night. We told them we were honest, innocent men, and abhorred such things; yet they apprehended us, and set a guard with halberds and pikes upon us that night, calling upon some of those Friendly people, with others, to watch us.

Next morning we were up betimes, and the constable, with his guard, carried us before a justice of the peace about five miles off. We took with us two or three of the sufficient men of the town, who had been with us at the great meeting at Captain Lawrence's, and could testify that we lay both the Seventh-day night and the First-day night at Captain Lawrence's;

and it was on the Seventh-day night that they said the house was broken into.

During the time that I was a prisoner in London ... this Captain Lawrence brought several Independent justices to see me there, with whom I had much discourse, at which they took offense. For they pleaded for imperfection, and to sin as long as they lived; but did not like to hear of Christ teaching His people Himself, and making people as clear, whilst here upon the earth, as Adam and Eve were before they fell. These justices had plotted together this mischief against me in the country, pretending that a house was broken into, that they might send their hue-and-cry after me....

... Providence so ordered that the constable carried us to a justice about five miles onward ... who ... began to be angry because we did not put off our hats to him. I told him I had been before the Protector, and he was not offended at my hat; and why should he be offended at it, who was but one of his servants? Then he read the hue-and-cry; and I told him that that night wherein the house was said to have been broken into, we were at Captain Lawrence's house and that we had several men present who could testify the truth thereof.

Thereupon the justice, having examined us and them, said he believed we were not the men that had broken into the house; but he was sorry, he said, that he had no more against us....

Being set at liberty, we passed on to Cambridge. When I came into the town the scholars, hearing of me, were up, and were exceeding rude. I kept on my horse's back, and rode through them in the Lord's power; but they unhorsed Amor Stoddart before he could get to the inn. . . . They knew I was so against the trade of preaching, which they were there as apprentices to learn, that they raged as greatly as ever Diana's craftsmen did against Paul. . . .

Next morning, having ordered our horses to be ready by the sixth hour, we passed peaceably out of town. The destroyers were disappointed: for they thought I would have stayed longer in the town, and intended to have done us mischief; but our passing away early in the morning frustrated their evil purposes against us.

At Evesham I heard that the magistrates had cast several Friends into diverse prisons, and that, hearing of my coming, they made a pair of high stocks.* I sent for Edward Pittaway, a Friend that lived near Evesham, and asked him the truth of the thing. He said it was so. I went that night with him to Evesham; and in the evening we had a large, precious meeting, wherein Friends and people were refreshed with the Word of life, the power of the Lord.

---

* Being put in stocks meant standing in public, bent over, with one's head and hands secured in strong wooden boards. It was meant to be both uncomfortable and humiliating.

Next morning I rode to one of the prisons, and visited Friends there, and encouraged them. Then I rode to the other prison, where were several prisoners. Amongst them was Humphry Smith, who had been a priest, but was now become a free minister of Christ. When I had visited Friends at both prisons, and was turned to go out of the town, I espied the magistrates coming up the town, intending to seize me in prison. . . .

Leaving Tewkesbury, we passed to Warwick, where in the evening we had a meeting with many sober people at a widow woman's house. A precious meeting we had in the Lord's power; several were convinced and turned to the Lord. After the meeting a Baptist in the company began to jangle; and the bailiff of the town, with his officers, came in and said, "What do these people here at this time of night?" So he secured John Crook, Amor Stoddart, Gerrard Roberts, and me; but we had leave to go to our inn, and to be forthcoming in the morning.

The next morning many rude people came into the inn, and into our chambers, desperate fellows; but the Lord's power gave us dominion over them. Gerrard Roberts and John Crook went to the bailiff to know what he had to say to us. He said we might go our ways, for he had little to say to us. As we rode out of town it lay upon me to ride to his house to let him know that, the Protector having given forth an

instrument of government in which liberty of conscience was granted, it was very strange that, contrary
to that instrument of government, he would trouble
peaceable people that feared God.

The Friends went with me, but the rude people
gathered about us with stones. One of them took hold
of my horse's bridle and broke it; but the horse, drawing back, threw him under him. Though the bailiff
saw this, yet he did not stop, nor so much as rebuke
the rude multitude; so that it was strange we were not
slain or hurt in the streets; for the people threw stones
and struck at us as we rode along the town.

When we were quite out of the town I told Friends
that it was upon me from the Lord that I must go
back into the town again; and if any one of them felt
anything upon him from the Lord he might follow
me; the rest, that did not, might go on.... So I passed
through the market in the dreadful power of God,
declaring the Word of life to them; and John Crook
followed me. Some struck at me; but the Lord's
power was over them, and gave me dominion over all.
I showed them their unworthiness to claim the name
of Christians, and the unworthiness of their teachers,
that had not brought them into more sobriety; and
what a shame they were to Christianity....

When we came to Baldock in Hertfordshire, I
asked if there was nothing in that town, no profession; and it was answered me that there were some

Baptists, and a Baptist woman who was sick. John Rush, of Bedfordshire, went with me to visit her.

. . . I was moved of the Lord God to speak to her; and the Lord raised her up again, to the astonishment of the town and country. This Baptist woman and her husband, whose name was Baldock, came to be convinced, and many hundreds of people have met at their house since. . . .

When we had visited this sick woman we returned to our inn, where were two desperate fellows fighting so furiously that none durst come nigh to part them. But I was moved, in the Lord's power, to go to them; and when I had loosed their hands, I held one of them by one hand and the other by the other, showed them the evil of their doings, and reconciled them one to the other; and they were so loving and thankful to me that people marveled at it. . . .*

Thence we went to Dorchester, and alighted at an inn, a Baptist's house. We sent into the town to the Baptists to ask them to let us have their meetinghouse to assemble in and to invite the sober people to the meeting; but they denied it us. We sent to them again, to know why they would deny us their meetinghouse, so the thing was noised about in the town. Then we sent them word that if they would not let us

---

* These cases are further illustration of Fox's power to deal with sickness and with desperate persons. He always *felt* himself equal to any emergency which confronted him.

come to their house, they, or any people that feared God, might come to our inn, if they pleased; but they were in a great rage. Their teacher and many of them came up, and slapped their Bibles on the table.

I asked them why they were so angry—"Were they angry with the Bible?" But they fell into a discourse about their water baptism. I asked them whether they could say they were sent of God to baptize people, as John was, and whether they had the same Spirit and power that the apostles had? They said they had not.

Then I asked them how many powers there are— whether there are any more than the power of God and the power of the devil. They said there was not any other power than those two. Then said I, "If you have not the power of God that the apostles had, you act by the power of the devil." Many sober people were present, who said they have thrown themselves on their backs. Many substantial people were convinced that night; a precious service we had there for the Lord and His power came over all. . . .

There was a captain of horse in the town, who sent to me, and would fain have had me stay longer; but I was not to stay. He and his man rode out of town with me about seven miles; Edward Pyot also being with me. This captain was the fattest, merriest, cheerfullest man, and the most given to laughter, that ever I met with: insomuch that I was several times moved to speak in the dreadful power of the Lord to him;

yet it was become so customary to him that he would presently laugh at anything he saw. But I still admonished him to come to sobriety, and the fear of the Lord and sincerity.

We lay at an inn that night, and the next morning I was moved to speak to him again, when he parted from us. The next time I saw him he told me that when I spoke to him at parting, the power of the Lord so struck him that before he got home he was serious enough, and discontinued his laughing. He afterwards was convinced, and became a serious and good man, and died in the Truth.

When we came to Ives, Edward Pyot's horse having cast a shoe, we stayed to have it set; and while he was getting his horse shod, I walked down to the seaside. When I returned I found the town in an uproar. They were haling Edward Pyot and the other Friend before Major Peter Ceely, a major in the army and a justice of the peace. I followed them into the justice's house, though they did not lay hands upon me.

When we came in, the house was full of rude people; whereupon I asked if there were not an officer among them to keep the people civil. Major Ceely said that he was a magistrate. I told him that he should then show forth gravity and sobriety, and use his authority to keep the people civil; for I never saw any people ruder; the Indians were more like Christians than they.

After awhile they brought forth a paper, and asked whether I would own it.* I said, Yes. Then he tendered the oath of abjuration† to us; whereupon I put my hand in my pocket and drew forth the answer to it which I had given to the Protector. After I had given him that, he examined us severally, one by one. He had with him a silly young priest, who asked us many frivolous questions; and amongst the rest he desired to cut my hair, which was then pretty long; but I was not to cut it, though many times many were offended at it. I told them I had no pride in it, and it was not of my own putting on.

At length the justice put us under a guard of soldiers, who were hard and wild, like the justice himself; nevertheless we warned the people of the day of the Lord, and declared the Truth to them. The next day he sent us, guarded by a party of horse with swords and pistols, to Redruth. On First-day the soldiers would have taken us away; but we told them it was their Sabbath, and it was not usual to travel on that day. . . .

In the afternoon the soldiers were resolved to take us away, so we took horse. When we were come to the town's end I was moved of the Lord to go back again, to speak to the old man of the house. The soldiers

---

* A paper which George Fox had written to the seven parishes of Land's End.
† Not to take up arms against Cromwell's government.

drew out their pistols, and swore I should not go back. I heeded them not, but rode back, and they rode after me. I cleared myself to the old man and the people, and then returned with them, and reproved them for being so rude and violent.

At night we were brought to a town then called Smethick, but since known as Falmouth. It being the evening of the First-day, there came to our inn the chief constable of the place, and many sober people, some of whom began to inquire concerning us. We told them we were prisoners for Truth's sake; and much discourse we had with them concerning the things of God. They were very sober and loving to us. Some were convinced, and stood faithful ever after.

When the constable and these people were gone, others came in, who were also very civil, and went away very loving. When all were gone, we went to our chamber to go to bed; and about the eleventh hour Edward Pyot said, "I will shut the door; it may be some may come to do us mischief." Afterwards we understood that Captain Keat, who commanded the party, had intended to do us some injury that night; but the door being bolted, he missed his design.

Next morning Captain Keat brought a kinsman of his, a rude, wicked man, and put him into the room; himself standing without. This evil-minded man walked huffing up and down the room; I bade him fear the Lord. Thereupon he ran upon me, struck me with both his hands, and, clapping his leg behind me, would have thrown me down if he could; but he was not able, for I stood stiff and still, and let him strike.

As I looked towards the door, I saw Captain Keat look on, and see his kinsman thus beat and abuse me. I said to him, "Keat, dost thou allow this?" He said he did. "Is this manly or civil," said I, "to have us under a guard, and then put a man to abuse and beat us? Is this manly, civil, or Christian?" I desired one of our friends to send for the constables, and they came.

Then I desired the Captain to let the constables see his warrant or order, by which he was to carry us; which he did. His warrant was to conduct us safe to Captain Fox, governor of Pendennis Castle; and if the governor should not be at home, he was to convey us to Launceston jail. I told him he had broken his order concerning us; for we, who were his prisoners, were to be safely conducted; but he had brought a man to beat and abuse us; so he having broken his order, I wished the constable to keep the warrant. Accordingly he did, and told the soldiers they might go their ways, for he would take charge of the prisoners; and if it cost twenty shillings in charges to carry us up, they should not have the warrant again. . . .

The constables went to the castle, and told the officers what they had done. The officers showed great dislike of Captain Keat's base carriage towards us; and told the constables that Major General Desborough was coming to Bodmin, and that we should meet him; and it was likely he would free us. Meanwhile our old guard of soldiers came by way of entreaty to us, and promised that they would be civil to us if we would go with them.

Thus the morning was spent till about the eleventh hour; and then, upon the soldiers' entreaty, and their promise to be more civil, the constables gave them the order again; and we went with them. . . .

Captain Keat, who commanded our guard, understanding that Captain Fox, who was governor of Pendennis Castle, was gone to meet Major General Desborough, did not carry us thither; but took us directly to Bodmin, in the way to Launceston. We met Major General Desborough on the way. The captain of his troop, who rode before him, knew me, and said, "Oh, Mr. Fox, what do you here?" I replied, "I am a prisoner." "Alack," he said, "for what?" I told him I was taken up as I was traveling. "Then," said he, "I will speak to my lord, and he will set you at liberty."

So he came from the head of his troop, and rode up to the coach, and spoke to the Major General. We also gave him an account of how we were taken. He began to speak against the Light of Christ; against which I exhorted him.* Then he told the soldiers that they

---

* Fox offends his would-be rescuer.

might carry us to Launceston; for he could not stay to talk with us, lest his horses should take cold. . . .

Next day we were brought to Launceston, where Captain Keat delivered us to the jailer. Now was there no Friend, nor Friendly people, near us; and the people of the town were a dark, hardened people. The jailer required us to pay seven shillings a week to feed our horses . . . and seven shillings a week apiece for our diet. After some time several sober persons came to see us, and some people of the town were convinced, and many friendly people out of several parts of the country came to visit us, and were convinced.

Then got up a great rage among the professors and priests against us. They said, "This people 'Thou' and 'Thee' all men without respect and will not put off their hats, nor bow the knee to any man; but we shall see, when the assize comes, whether they will dare to 'Thou' and 'Thee' the judge, and keep on their hats before him." They expected we should be hanged at the assize. . . .

It was nine weeks from the time of our commitment to the time of the assizes, to which abundance of people came from far and near to hear the trial of the Quakers. Captain Bradden lay there with his troop of horse. His soldiers and the sheriff's men guarded us to the court through the multitude that filled the streets; and much ado they had to get us through. Besides, the doors and windows were filled with people looking upon us.

When we were brought into the court, we stood awhile with our hats on, and all was quiet. I was moved to say, "Peace be amongst you."

Judge Glynne, a Welshman, then Chief Justice of England, said to the jailer, "What be these you have brought here into the court?" "Prisoners, my lord," said he.

"Why do you not put off your hats?" said the Judge to us. We said nothing.

"Put off your hats," said the Judge again. Still we said nothing. Then said the Judge, "The Court commands you to put off your hats."

Then I spoke, and said, "Where did ever any magistrate, king, or judge, from Moses to Daniel, command any to put off their hats, when they came before him in his court, either amongst the Jews, the people of God, or amongst the heathen? And if the law of England doth command any such thing, show me that law either written or printed."

Then the Judge grew very angry, and said, "I do not carry my law books on my back." "But," said I, "tell me where it is printed in any statute book, that I may read it."

Then said the Judge, "Take him away, prevaricator! I'll *ferk** him." So they took us away, and put us among the thieves.

---

* To whip, to chastise.

Presently after he calls to the jailer, "Bring them up again." "Come," said he, "where had they hats, from Moses to Daniel; come, answer me: I have you fast now."

I replied, "Thou mayest read in the third of Daniel, that the three children were cast into the fiery furnace by Nebuchadnezzar's command, with their coats, their hose, and their hats on."*

This plain instance stopped him: so that, not having anything else to say to the point, he cried again, "Take them away, jailer. . . ."

We had some good books to set forth our principles, and to inform people of the Truth. The Judge and justices hearing of this, they sent Captain Bradden for them. He came into the jail to us, and violently took our books from us, some out of Edward Pyot's hands, and carried them away; so we never got them again.

[While in the jail Fox addressed a paper "against swearing" to the grand and petty juries.] This paper passing among them from the jury to the justices, they presented it to the Judge; so that when we were called before the Judge, he bade the clerk give me that paper, and then asked me whether that seditious paper was mine. I said to him, "If they will read it out in open court, that I may hear it, if it is mine I will own it, and stand by it." He would have had me take it and look

---

* Fox's complete command of the Bible again confounds his enemies, because the Bible represented an irrefutable authority in Puritan England.

upon it in my own hand; but I again desired that it might be read, that all the country might hear it, and judge whether there was any sedition in it or not; for if there were, I was willing to suffer for it.

At last the clerk of the assize read it, with an audible voice, that all the people might hear it. When he had done I told them it was my paper; that I would own it, and so might they too, unless they would deny the Scripture: for was not this Scripture language, and the words and commands of Christ, and the Apostle, which all true Christians ought to obey?

Then they let fall that subject; and the Judge fell upon us about our hats again, bidding the jailer take them off; which he did, and gave them to us; and we put them on again.* Then we asked the Judge and the justices, for what cause we had lain in prison these nine weeks, seeing they now objected to nothing but our hats. And as for putting off our hats, I told them that that was the honor which God would lay in the dust, though they made so much ado about it; the honor which is of men, and which men seek one of another, and is a mark of unbelievers. For "How can ye believe," saith Christ, "who receive honor one of another, and seek not the honor that cometh from God only?" Christ saith,

---

* Fox never compromised his principles, no matter what the consequences were.

"I receive not honor from men"; and all true Christians should be of His mind.*

Then the Judge began to make a pompous speech, how he represented the Lord Protector's person, who made him Lord Chief Justice of England, and sent him to come that circuit, etc. We desired him, then, that he would do us justice for our false imprisonment which we had suffered nine weeks wrongfully. But instead of that, they brought an indictment framed against us; so full of lies that I thought it had been against some of the thieves—"that we came by force and arms, and in a hostile manner, into the court"; who were brought as aforesaid. I told them it was all false; and still we cried for justice for our false imprisonment, being taken up in our journey without cause by Major Ceely.

Then Peter Ceely said to the Judge, "May it please you, my lord, this man (pointing to me) went aside with me, and told me how serviceable I might be for his design; that he could raise forty thousand men at an hour's warning, involve the nation in blood, and so bring in King Charles. I would have aided him out of the country, but he would not go. If it please you, my lord, I have a witness to swear it."

So he called upon his witness; but the Judge not being forward to examine the witness, I desired that he would be pleased to let my mittimus be read in

---

* Now Fox is citing Jesus, the highest authority.

the face of the court and the country, in which the crime was signified for which I was sent to prison. The Judge said it should not be read. I said, "It ought to be, seeing it concerned my liberty and my life." The Judge said again, "It shall not be read." I said, "It ought to be read; for if I have done anything worthy of death, or of bonds, let all the country know it."

Then seeing they would not read it, I spoke to one of my fellow prisoners: "Thou hast a copy of it; read it up." "It shall not be read," said the Judge; "Jailer, take him away. I'll see whether he or I shall be master."

So I was taken away and awhile after called for again. I still called to have the mittimus read; for that signified the cause of my commitment. I again spoke to the Friend, my fellow prisoner, to read it up; which he did. The Judge, justices, and the whole court were silent; for the people were eager to hear it. It was as followeth:

> Peter Ceely, one of the justices of the peace of this county, to the keeper of His Highness's jail at Launceston, or his lawful deputy in that behalf, greeting:

> I send you here withal by the bearers hereof, the bodies of Edward Pyot, of Bristol, and George Fox, of Drayton-in-the-Clay, in Leicestershire, and William Salt, of London, which they pretend to be the places of their habitations, who go under the notion

of Quakers, and acknowledge themselves to be such; who have spread several papers tending to the disturbance of the public peace, and cannot render any lawful cause of coming into those parts, being persons altogether unknown, having no pass for traveling up and down the country, and refusing to give sureties for their good behavior, according to the law in that behalf provided; and refuse to take oath of abjuration, etc. These are, therefore, in the name of his highness the Lord Protector, to will and command you, that when the bodies of the said Edward Pyot, George Fox, and William Salt, shall be unto you brought, you them receive, and in His Highness's prison aforesaid you safely keep them, until by due course of law they shall be delivered. Hereof fail you not, as you will answer the contrary at your perils. Given under my hand and seal, at St. Ives, the 18th day of January, 1655.

P. Ceely

When it was read I spoke thus to the Judge and justices:

Thou that sayest thou art Chief Justice of England, and you justices, know that, if I had put in sureties, I might have gone whither I pleased, and have carried on the design (if I had had one) with which Major Ceely hath charged me. . . .

Then, turning my speech to Major Ceely, I said:

When or where did I take thee aside? Was not thy house full of rude people, and thou as rude as any of them, at our examination; so that I asked for a constable or some other officer to keep the people civil? But if thou art my accuser, why sittest thou on the bench? It is not the place of accusers to sit with the judge. Thou oughtest to come down and stand by me, and look me in the face.

Besides, I would ask the Judge and justices whether Major Ceely is not guilty of this treason, which he charges against me, in concealing it so long as he hath done? Does he understand his place, either as a soldier or a justice of the peace? For he tells you here that I went aside with him, and told him what a design I had in hand, and how serviceable he might be for my design: that I could raise forty thousand men in an hour's time, bring in King Charles, and involve the nation in blood. He saith, moreover, that he would have aided me out of the country, but I would not go; and therefore he committed me to prison for want of sureties for the good behavior, as the mittimus declares.

Now, do you not see plainly that Major Ceely is guilty of this plot and treason he talks of, and hath made himself a party to it by desiring me to go out of the country, demanding bail of me, and not charging me with this pretended treason till now, nor discovering it? But I deny and abhor his words, and am innocent of his devilish design.

So that business was let fall; for the Judge saw clearly enough that instead of ensnaring me, Major Ceely had ensnared himself.

Major Ceely got up again, and said, "If it please you, my lord, to hear me: this man struck me, and gave me such a blow as I never had in my life." At this I smiled in my heart, and said, "Major Ceely, art thou a justice of the peace, and a major of a troop of horse, and tellest the Judge, in the face of the court and country, that I, a prisoner, struck thee and gave thee such a blow as thou never hadst the like in thy life? What! Art thou not ashamed? Prithee, Major Ceely," said I, "Where did I strike thee? And who is thy witness for that? Who was by?"

He said it was in the Castle-Green, and Captain Bradden was standing by when I struck him. I desired the Judge to let him produce his witness for that; and called again upon Major Ceely to come down from the bench, telling him that it was not fit that the accuser should sit as judge over the accused. When I called again for his witness, he said that Captain Bradden was his witness.

Then I said, "Speak, Captain Bradden, didst thou see me give him such a blow, and strike him as he saith?" Captain Bradden made no answer; but bowed his head towards me. I desired him to speak up, if he knew any such thing; but he only bowed his head again. "Nay," said I, "speak up, and let the court and country hear, and let not bowing of the head serve the turn. If I have done so, let the law be inflicted on me; I fear not sufferings, nor death itself, for I am an innocent man concerning all this charge."

But Captain Bradden never testified to it; and the Judge, finding those snares would not hold, cried, "Take him away, jailer"; and then, when we were taken away, he fined us twenty marks apiece for not putting off our hats; and sentenced us to be kept in prison till we paid it; so he sent us back to the jail. . . .

The assizes being over, and we settled in prison upon such a commitment that we were not likely to be soon released, we broke off from giving the jailer seven shillings a week apiece for our horses, and seven shillings a week for ourselves, and sent our horses into the country. Upon which he grew very wicked and devilish, and put us down into Doomsdale, a nasty, stinking place, where they used to put murderers after they were condemned.

The place was so noisome that it was observed few that went in did ever come out again in health. There was no latrine … in it; and the excrement of the prisoners that from time to time had been put there had not been carried out (as we were told) for many years. So that it was all like mire, and in some places to the tops of the shoes in water and urine; and he would not let us cleanse it, nor suffer us to have beds or straw to lie on.

At night some friendly people of the town brought us a candle and a little straw; and we burned a little of our straw to take away the stink. The thieves lay over our heads, and the head jailer in a room by them, over our heads also. It seems the smoke went up into the room where the jailer lay; which put him into such a rage that he took the pots of excrement from the thieves and poured them through a hole upon our heads in Doomsdale, till we were so bespattered that we could not touch ourselves nor one another. And the stink increased upon us; so that what with stink, and what with smoke, we were almost choked and smothered. We had the stink under our feet before, but now we had it on our heads and backs also; and he having quenched our straw with the filth he poured down, had made a great smother in the place. Moreover, he railed at us most hideously, calling us hatchet-faced dogs, and such strange names as we had never heard of. In this manner we were obliged to stand all night, for we could not sit down, the place was so full of filthy excrement.

A great while he kept us after this manner before he would let us cleanse it, or suffer us to have any victuals brought in but what we got through the grate. One time a girl brought us a little meat; and he arrested her for breaking into his house, and sued her in the town court for breaking into the prison. A great deal of trouble he put the young woman to; whereby others were so discouraged that we had much ado to get water, drink, or victuals. . . .

By this time the general quarter sessions drew nigh; and the jailer still carrying himself basely and wickedly towards us, we drew up our suffering case, and sent it to the sessions at Bodmin. On the reading thereof, the justices gave order that Doomsdale door should be opened, and that we should have liberty to cleanse it, and to buy our meat in the town. We also sent a copy of our sufferings to the Protector, setting forth how we had been taken and committed by Major Ceely; and abused by Captain Keat as aforesaid, and the rest in order. The Protector sent down an order to Captain Fox, governor of Pendennis Castle, to examine the matter about the soldiers abusing us, and striking me.

There were at that time many of the gentry of the country at the Castle; and Captain Keat's kinsman, who . . . struck me, was sent for before them, and much threatened. They told him that if I should change my principles, I might take the extremity of the law against him, and might recover sound damages of him. Captain Keat also was checked, for suffering the prisoners under his charge to be abused.

This was of great service in the country; for afterwards Friends might speak in any market or steeple-house thereabouts, and none would meddle with them. I understood that Hugh Peters, one of the Protector's chaplains, told him they could not do George Fox a greater service for the spreading of his principles in Cornwall, than to imprison him there.

And indeed my imprisonment there was of the Lord, and for His service in those parts; for after the assizes were over, and it was known that we were likely to continue prisoners, several Friends from most parts of the nation came into the country to visit us. Those parts of the west were very dark countries at that time but the Lord's light and truth broke forth, shone over all, and many were turned from darkness to light, and from Satan's power unto God. Many were moved to go to the steeple-houses; and several were sent to prison to us; and a great convincement began in the country. For now we had liberty to come out and to walk in the Castle-Green; and many came to us on First-days, to whom we declared the Word of life. . . .

Another time, about eleven at night, the jailer, being half drunk, came and told me that he had got a man now to dispute with me (this was when we had leave to go a little into the town). As soon as he spoke these words I felt there was mischief intended to my body....

Then I rose and walked into the Castle-Green, and the under-keeper came and told me that there was a maid would speak with me in the prison. I felt a snare in his words, too, therefore I went not into the prison, but to the grate; and looking in, I saw a man who ... was lately brought to prison for being a conjurer, who had a naked knife in his hand. I spoke to him, and he threatened to cut my chaps; but, being within the jail he could not come at me. This was the jailer's great disputant.

I went soon after into the jailer's house, and found him at breakfast; he had then got his conjurer out with him. I told the jailer his plot was discovered. Then he got up from the table, and cast his napkin away in a rage; and I left them, and went to my chamber; for at this time we were out of Doomsdale.

At the time the jailer had said the dispute should be, I went down and walked in the court (the place appointed) till about the eleventh hour; but nobody came. Then I went up to my chamber again; and after awhile heard one call for me. I stepped to the stairs head, where I saw the jailer's wife upon the stairs, and the conjurer at the bottom of the stairs, holding his hand behind his back, and in a great rage.

I asked him, "Man, what hast thou in thy hand behind thy back? Pluck thy hand before thee," said I; "Let's see thy hand, and what thou hast in it."

Then he angrily plucked forth his hand, with a naked knife in it. I showed the jailer's wife their wicked design against me; for this was the man they brought to dispute of the things of God. But the Lord discovered their plot, and prevented their evil design; and they both raged, and the conjurer threatened.

Then I was moved of the Lord to speak sharply to him in the dreadful power of the Lord; and the Lord's power came over him, and bound him down; so that he never after durst appear before me. . . . I saw it was the Lord alone who . . . had preserved me out of their bloody hands; for the devil had a great enmity to me, and stirred up his instruments to seek my hurt. But the Lord prevented them; and my heart was filled with thanksgivings and praises to him.

In Cornwall, Devonshire, Dorsetshire, and Somersetshire, Truth began mightily to spread. Many were turned to Christ Jesus and His free teaching: for many Friends that came to visit us were drawn to declare the Truth in those counties. This made the priests and professors rage, and they stirred up the magistrates to ensnare Friends. They set up watches in the streets and highways, on pretense of taking up suspicious persons, under which color they stopped and took up Friends coming to visit us in prison;

which was done that these Friends might not pass up and down in the Lord's service.

But that by which they thought to have stopped the Truth was the means of spreading it so much the more; for then Friends were frequently moved to speak to one constable and to another officer, and to the justices before whom they were brought; which caused the Truth to spread the more in all their parishes. And when Friends were got among the watches, it would be a fortnight or three weeks before they could get out of them again; for no sooner had one constable taken and carried them before the justices, and these had discharged them, but another would take them up and carry them before other justices: which put the country to a great deal of needless trouble and charges.

... Many Friends were cruelly beaten by them; nay, some clothiers that were but going to mill with their cloth, and others about their occupations ..., they took up and whipped; though men of about eighty or a hundred pounds by the year in income, a large sum, and not above four or five miles from their families.

While I was in prison here, the Baptists and Fifth Monarchy Men prophesied that this year Christ should come, and reign upon earth a thousand years. And they looked upon this reign to be outward: when [in Fox's teaching] He was already come inwardly in the hearts of His people, to reign and rule; where these professors would not receive Him. So they failed in their prophecy and expectation, and had not the possession of Him. But Christ is already come, and doth dwell and reign in the hearts of His people. . . .

Thomas Lower, Judge Fell's son-in-law, also came to visit us, and offered us money, which we refused; accepting nevertheless of his love. . . .

. . . The jailer was very bad himself; I often admonished him to sobriety; but he abused people that came to visit us. Edward Pyot had a cheese sent him from Bristol by his wife; and the jailer took it from him, and carried it to the mayor, to search it for treasonable letters, as he said; and though they found no treason in the cheese, they kept it from us. This jailer might have been rich—if he had carried himself civilly; but he sought his own ruin, which soon after came upon him.

The next year he was turned out of his place, and for some wickedness cast into the jail himself; and there begged of our Friends. And for some unruliness in his conduct he was, by the succeeding jailer, put into Doomsdale, locked in irons, and beaten, and bidden to remember how he had abused those good men whom he had wickedly, without any cause, cast into that nasty dungeon; and told that now he deservedly should suffer for his wickedness; and the same measure he had meted to others, should be meted out to himself. He became very poor, . . . died in prison; and his wife and family came to misery. . . .

. . . In the meantime, . . . Colonel Bennet, who had the command of the jail, . . . would have set us at liberty if we would have paid his jailer's fees. But we told him we could give the jailer no fees, for we were innocent sufferers; and how could they expect fees of us, who had suffered so long wrongfully? After awhile Colonel Bennet coming to town, sent for us to an inn, and insisted again upon fees, which we refused. At last the power of the Lord came so over him, that he freely set us at liberty on the 13th day of the Seventh month, 1656. . . .

Chapter Ten

Planting the Seed in Wales

(1656–1657)

S OON AFTER WE came to Exeter, where many Friends were in prison; and amongst the rest James Nayler. For a little before we were set at liberty, James had run out into imaginations,* and a company with him, who raised a great darkness in the nation. He came to Bristol, and made a disturbance there....

The night that we came to Exeter I spoke with James Nayler: for I saw he was out, and wrong, and so was his company....

---

* His mind had betrayed him, possibly because of constant hardship and suffering, and he began to think he was Jesus.

The next day I spoke to James Nayler again; and he slighted what I said, was dark, and much out; yet he would have come and kissed me. But I said that since he had turned against the power of God, I could not receive his show of kindness. The Lord moved me to slight him, and to set the power of God over him. So after I had been warring with the world, there was now a wicked spirit risen amongst Friends to war against. I admonished him and his company.

. . . But he came to see his out-going, and to condemn it; and after some time he returned to Truth again; as in the printed relation of his repentance, condemnation, and recovery. . . .*

Soon after we rode to London. When we came near Hyde Park we saw a great concourse of people, and, looking towards them, espied the Protector (Oliver Cromwell) coming in his coach. Whereupon I rode to his coach side. Some of his life-guard would have put me away; but he forbade them. So I rode by his coach side with him, declaring what the Lord gave me to say to him, of his condition, and of the sufferings of Friends in the nation, showing him how contrary this persecution was to the words of Christ and His apostles, and to Christianity. . . .

---

* Although not before he had been publicly tortured by the civil authorities (his tongue was pierced by a red hot iron among many other punishments). His death followed shortly thereafter. The Naylor episode was a major setback for the Friends.

After a little time Edward Pyot and I went to Whitehall to see Oliver Cromwell; and when we came before him, Dr. Owen, vice chancellor of Oxford, was with him. We were moved to speak to him concerning the sufferings of Friends, and laid them before him: and we directed him to the Light of Christ, who had enlightened every man that cometh into the world. He said ours was a natural light; but we showed him the contrary; and proved that it was divine and spiritual, proceeding from Christ the spiritual and heavenly man. . . .

The power of the Lord God arose in me, and I was moved in it to bid him lay down his crown at the feet of Jesus. Several times I spoke to him to the same effect. I was standing by the table, and he came and sat upon the table's side by me, saying he would be as high as I was. So he continued speaking against the Light of Christ Jesus; and went his way in a light manner. . . .

. . . Having traveled over most of the nation, I returned to London again, having cleared myself of that which lay upon me from the Lord. For after I was released out of Launceston jail, I was moved of the Lord to travel over the nation, the Truth being now spread in most places, that I might answer, and remove out of the minds of the people, some objections which the envious priests and professors had raised and spread abroad concerning us.

In this year the Lord's Truth was finely planted over the nation, and many thousands were turned to the Lord; insomuch that there were seldom fewer than one thousand in prison in this nation for Truth's testimony; some for not paying tithes to support the established church, some for going to the steeple-houses to preach, some for contempts (as they called them), some for not swearing, and others for not putting off their hats. . . .

We lay one night at Farnham, where we had a little meeting. The people were exceeding rude; but at last the Lord's power came over them. After meeting we went to our inn, and gave notice that any who feared God might come to our inn to us. . . .

. . . A rude company of professors came up, and some of the chief of the town. They called for faggots and drink, though we forbade them, and were as rude a people as ever I met. The Lord's power chained them, that they had not power to do us any mischief; but when they went away they left all the faggots and beer, for which they had called, in the room, for us to pay for in the morning. We showed the innkeeper what an unworthy thing it was; but he told us we must pay it; and pay it we did. . . .

We passed through the counties in Wales having meetings, and gathering people in the name of Christ, their heavenly teacher . . . and so into Radnorshire. . . .

When they were well gathered, I went into the meeting, and stood upon a chair about three hours. I stood a pretty while before I began to speak. After some time I felt the power of the Lord over the whole assembly: and His everlasting life and Truth shone over all. . . .*

From this place I traveled on in Wales,† having several meetings, till I came to Tenby, where, as I rode up the street, a justice of the peace came out to me, asked me to alight, and desired that I would stay at his house, which I did. . . .

John ap-John being then with me, left the meeting, and went to the steeple-house; and the governor cast him into prison. On Second-day morning the governor sent one of his officers to the justice's to fetch me; which grieved the mayor and the justice; for they were both with me in the justice's house when the officer came. The mayor and the justice went to the governor before me; and awhile after I went with the officer. When I came in I said, "Peace be unto this house," and before the governor could examine me I asked him why he cast my friend into prison. He said, "For standing with his hat on in the church."

I said, "Had not the priest two caps on his head, a black one and a white one? Cut off the brims of the hat, and then my friend would have but one: and the brims of the hat were but to defend him from weather."

---

* This is an example of what became the style at Friends Meetings on Sunday. The congregants would wait until someone was inspired by an inner voice, identified with that of Jesus, to speak.

† Many Welsh Friends emigrated to Pennsylvania.

"These are frivolous things," said the governor.

"Why, then," said I, "dost thou cast my friend into prison for such frivolous things?"

He asked me whether I owned election and reprobation.* "Yes," said I, "and thou art in the reprobation."

At that he was in a rage and said he would send me to prison till I proved it. I told him I would prove that quickly if he would confess Truth. I asked him whether wrath, fury, rage, and persecution were not marks of reprobation; for he that was born of the flesh persecuted him that was born of the Spirit; but Christ and His disciples never persecuted nor imprisoned any.

He fairly confessed that he had too much wrath, haste, and passion in him. I told him that Esau was up in him, the first birth; not Jacob, the second birth. The Lord's power so reached the man and came over him that he confessed to Truth; and the other justice came and shook me kindly by the hand.

As I was passing away I was moved to speak to the governor again; and he invited me to dinner with him, and set my friend at liberty. . . .

After this we passed into another county, and at noon came into a great market town, and went into several inns before we could get any food . . . for our horses. At last we came to one where we got some. Then John ap-John being with me went and spoke through

---

* Damnation.

the town, declaring the Truth to the people; and when he came to me again, he said he thought all the town were as people asleep. After awhile he was moved to go and declare Truth in the streets again; then the town was all in an uproar, and they cast him into prison....

After we had refreshed ourselves a little, and were ready, we took horse, and rode up to the inn, where the mayor, sheriff, and justices were. I called to speak with them, and asked them why they had imprisoned John ap-John, and kept him in prison two or three hours. But they would not answer me a word; they only looked out at the windows upon me. So I showed them how unchristian was their carriage to strangers and travelers, and how it manifested the fruits of their teachers; and I declared the truth unto them, and warned them of the day of the Lord, that was coming upon all evildoers; and the Lord's power came over them, that they looked ashamed; but not a word could I get from them in answer.

So when I had warned them to repent, and turn to the Lord, we passed away....

Next day, being market day, we were to cross a great water.... There we tarried, from the eleventh hour of the forenoon to the second in the afternoon, before the boat came to fetch us; and then had forty-two miles to ride that evening; and by the time we had paid for our passage, we had but one groat left between us in money.

We rode about sixteen miles, and then got a little hay for our horses. Setting forward again, we came in the night to a little alehouse, where we thought to have stayed. . . . But, finding we could have neither oats nor hay there, we traveled all night; and about the fifth hour in the morning got to a place within six miles of Wrexham, where that day we met with many Friends, and had a glorious meeting. The Lord's everlasting power and Truth was over all; and a meeting is continued there to this day. . . .

From Wrexham we came to Chester; and it being the fair time, we stayed awhile, and visited Friends. For I had traveled through every county in Wales, preaching the everlasting gospel of Christ; and a brave people there is now, who have received it, and sit under Christ's teaching. . . .

Chapter Eleven

In the Home of the Covenanters

(1657)

I HAD FOR SOME time felt drawings on my spirit to go into Scotland, and had sent to Colonel William Osburn of Scotland, desiring him to meet me; and he, with some others, came out of Scotland to this meeting.* After it was over (which, he said, was the most glorious meeting that ever he saw in his life), I passed with him and his company into Scotland, having with me Robert Widders, a thundering man against hypocrisy, deceit, and the rottenness of the priests. . . .

---

* In Anglesey, Cumberland.

On First-day we had a great meeting, and several professors came to it. Now, the priests had frightened the people with the doctrine of election and reprobation, telling them that God had ordained the greatest part of men and women for hell; and that, let them pray, or preach, or sing, or do what they would, it was all to no purpose, if they were ordained for hell. Also that God had a certain number elected for heaven, let them do what they would; as David was an adulterer, and Paul a persecutor, yet still they were elected vessels for heaven. So the priests said the fault was not at all in the creature, less or more, but that God had ordained it so.

I was led to open to the people the falseness and folly of their priests' doctrines and showed how they, the priests, had abused those Scriptures they quoted. Now all that believe in the Light of Christ, as He commands, are in the election, and sit under the teaching of the grace of God, which brings their salvation. But such as turn this grace into wantonness, are in the reprobation; and such as hate the Light, are in the condemnation.

So I exhorted all the people to believe in the Light, as Christ commands, and to own the grace of God, their free teacher; and it would assuredly bring them their salvation; for it is sufficient. Many Scriptures were opened concerning reprobation, and the eyes of the people were opened; and a spring of life rose up among them.

These things soon came to the priest's ears; for the people that sat under their dark teachings began to see light, and to come into the covenant of light. The noise was spread over Scotland, amongst the priests, that I was come thither; and a great cry went up among them that all would be spoiled; for, they said, I had spoiled all the honest men and women in England already; so, according to their own account, the worst were left to them. . . .

Now were the priests in such a rage that they posted to Edinburgh to Oliver Cromwell's Council there, with petitions against me. . . .

. . . I went on to Edinburgh. . . . Many thousands were gathered together, with abundance of priests among them, about burning a witch, and I was moved to declare the day of the Lord amongst them. When I had done, I went thence to our meeting, whither came many rude people and Baptists.

The Baptists began to vaunt with their logic and syllogisms; but I was moved in the Lord's power to thresh their chaffy, light minds. I showed the people that, after that fallacious way of discoursing, they might make white seem black, and black seem white; as, that because a cock had two legs, and each of them had two legs, therefore they were all cocks. Thus they might turn anything into lightness and vanity; but it was not the way of Christ, or His apostles, to teach, speak, or reason after that manner.

Hereupon those Baptists went their way; and after they were gone we had a blessed meeting in the Lord's power, which was over all.

... When I came from the meeting to the inn where I lodged, an officer belonging to the Council brought me the following order:

> Thursday, the 8th of October, 1657, at his Highness' Council in Scotland:
>
> Ordered, That George Fox do appear before the Council on Tuesday, the 13th of October next, in the forenoon.
>
> —E. Downing, Clerk of the Council

... When the time came I appeared, and was taken into a great room, where many persons came and looked at me. After awhile the doorkeeper took me into the council chamber; and as I was going he took off my hat. I asked him why he did so, and who was there that I might not go in with my hat on. I told him I had been before the Protector with my hat on. But he hung up my hat and took me in before them.

When I had stood awhile, and they said nothing to me, I was moved of the Lord to say, "Peace be amongst you. Wait in the fear of God, that ye may receive His wisdom from above, by which all things were made and created; that by it ye may all be ordered, and may order all things under your hands to God's glory."

They asked me what was the occasion of my coming into that nation. I told them I came to visit the Seed of God, which had long lain in bondage under corruption, so that all in the nation who professed the Scriptures, the words of Christ, of the prophets and apostles, might come to the Light, Spirit and power, which they were in who gave them forth. I told them that in and by the Spirit they might understand the Scriptures, and know Christ and God aright, and might have fellowship with them, and one with another.

They asked me whether I had any outward business there. I said, "Nay." Then they asked me how long I intended to stay in that country. I told them I should say little to that; my time was not to be long; yet in my freedom in the Lord I stood, in the will of Him that sent me.

Then they bade me withdraw, and the doorkeeper took me by the hand and led me forth. In a little time they sent for me again, and told me that I must depart the nation of Scotland by that day seven-night. I asked them, "Why? What have I done? What is my transgression that you pass such a sentence upon me to depart out of the nation?" They told me they would not dispute with me. I desired them to hear what I had to say to them. They said they would not hear me. I told them, "Pharaoh heard Moses and Aaron, yet he was a heathen; and Herod heard John the Baptist; and you should not be worse than these." But they cried, "Withdraw, withdraw." Thereupon the door-keeper took me again by the hand and led me out.

I returned to my inn, and continued still in Edin-burgh; visiting Friends there and thereabouts, and strengthening them in the Lord. After a little time I wrote a letter to the Council to lay before them their unchristian dealings in banishing me, an innocent man, that sought their salvation and eternal good.

After I had spent some time among Friends at Edinburgh and thereabouts, I passed thence to Heads again, where Friends had been in great sufferings. For the Presbyterian priests had excommunicated them, and given charge that none should buy or sell or eat or drink with them. So they could neither sell their commodities nor buy what they wanted; which made it go very hard with some of them; for if they had bought bread or other victuals of any of their neigh-bors, the priests threatened them so with curses that they would run and fetch it from them again. But Colonel Ashfield, being a justice of the peace in that country, put a stop to the priests' proceedings. This Colonel Ashfield was afterwards convinced himself, had a meeting settled at his house, declared the Truth, and lived and died in it. . . .

We traveled . . . to Leith, warning and exhorting people, as we went, to turn to the Lord. At Leith the innkeeper told me that the Council had granted war-rants to apprehend me, because I was not gone out of the nation after the seven days were expired that they had ordered me to depart in. Several friendly people also came and told me the same; to whom I said, "Why do ye tell me of their warrants against me? If there were a cartload of them I would not heed them, for the Lord's power is over them all."

I went from Leith to Edinburgh again, where they said the warrants from the Council were out against me. I went to the inn where I had lodged before, and no man offered to meddle with me. After I had visited Friends in the city, I desired those that traveled with me to get ready their horses in the morning, and we rode out of town together. There were with me at that time Thomas Rawlinson, Alexander Parker, and Robert Widders.

When we were out of town they asked me whither I would go. I told them it was upon me from the Lord to go back again to Johnstons (the town out of which we had been lately thrust), to set the power of God and His Truth over them also. . . .

. . . I rode up the street to Captain Davenport's house, from which we had been banished. There were many officers with him; and when I came amongst them they lifted up their hands, wondering that I should come again. But I told them the Lord God had sent me amongst them again; so they went their way. . . .

This Captain Davenport was then loving to Friends; and afterwards, coming more into obedience to Truth, he was turned out of his place for not putting off his hat, and for saying Thou and Thee to them. . . .

. . . The next day, being Second-day, we set forward towards the borders of England. . . .

Chapter Twelve
Great Events in London
(1658–1659)

W E CAME INTO Bedfordshire, where we had large gatherings in the name of Jesus. After some time we came to John Crook's at Luton, in Bedfordshire where a general yearly meeting for the whole nation was appointed to be held. . . .

After this meeting was over, and most of the Friends gone away, as I was walking in John Crook's garden, there came a party of horse, with a constable, to seize me. I heard them ask, "Who is in the house?" Somebody made answer that I was there. They said that I was the man they looked for; and went forthwith into the house, where they had many words with John Crook and some few Friends that were with him. But the Lord's power so confounded them that they came not into the garden to look for me; but went their way in a rage.

When I came into the house, Friends were very glad to see that I had escaped them. Next day I passed thence; and, after I had visited Friends in several places, came to London, the Lord's power accompanying me, and bearing me up in His service.

During the time I was at London I had many services laid upon me, for it was a time of much suffering. I was moved to write to Oliver Cromwell, and lay before him the sufferings of Friends both in this nation and in Ireland. There was also a talk about this time of making Cromwell king; whereupon I was moved to go to him and warn him against accepting it; and of diverse dangers which, if he did not avoid them, would, I told him, bring shame and ruin upon himself and his posterity. He seemed to take well what I said to him, and thanked me; yet afterwards I was moved to write to him more fully concerning that matter. . . .

About this time came forth a declaration from Oliver Cromwell, the Protector, for a collection towards the relief of diverse Protestant churches, driven out of Poland; and of twenty Protestant families, driven out of the confines of Bohemia. And there was . . . a like declaration published some time before, to invite the nation to a day of solemn fasting and humiliation, in order to . . . contribute . . . for the suffering Protestants

of the valleys of Lucerne, Angrona, etc., who were persecuted by the Duke of Savoy, I was moved to write to
the Protector and chief magistrates on this occasion,
both to show them the nature of a true fast (such as
God requires and accepts), and to make them sensible of their injustice and self-condemnation in blam-
ing the Papists for persecuting the Protestants abroad,
while they themselves, calling themselves Protestants,
were at the same time persecuting their Protestant
neighbors and friends at home.

Diverse times, both in the time of the Long Parliament and of the Protector (so called) and of the
Committee of Safety, when they proclaimed fasts,
I was moved to write to them, and tell them their
fasts were like unto Jezebel's; for commonly, when
they proclaimed fasts, there was some mischief con-
trived against us. I knew their fasts were for strife
and debate, to smite with the fist of wickedness; as
the New England professors soon after did; who,
before they put our Friends to death, proclaimed a
fast also.

Now it was a time of great suffering; and many
Friends being in prisons, many other Friends were
moved to go to the Parliament, to offer themselves
up to lie in the same prisons where their friends lay,
that those in prison might go forth, and not perish
in the stinking jails. This we did in love to God and
our brethren, that they might not die in prison; and

in love to those that cast them in, that they might not bring innocent blood upon their own heads, which we knew would cry to the Lord, and bring His wrath, vengeance, and plagues upon them. . . .

And because the Parliament that now sat* was made up mostly of high professors, who, pretending to be more religious than others, were indeed greater persecutors of those that were truly religious, I was moved to send them the following lines, as a reproof of their hypocrisy. . . .

> O friends, do not cloak and cover yourselves; there is a God that knoweth your hearts, and that will uncover you. He seeth your way. . . . My Savior spoke against such; 'I was sick, and ye visited me not; I was hungry, and ye fed me not; I was a stranger, and ye took me not in; I was in prison, and ye visited me not.' But they said, 'When saw we thee in prison, and did not come to thee?' 'Inasmuch as ye did it not unto one of these little ones, ye did it not unto me.' Friends, ye imprison them that are in the life and power of Truth, and yet profess to be the ministers of Christ. . . .

> G. F.

---

* Cromwell's *Second Parliament.*

... Taking boat, I went to Kingston near London, and thence to Hampton Court, to speak with the Protector about the sufferings of Friends. I met him riding in Hampton Court Park, and before I came to him, as he rode at the head of his life-guard, I saw and felt a waft [or apparition] of death go forth against him; and when I came to him he looked like a dead man.

After I had laid the sufferings of Friends before him, and had warned him, according as I was moved to speak to him, he bade me come to his house. So I returned to Kingston, and next day went to Hampton Court, to speak further with him. But when I came he was sick, and—his bed attendant, Harvey, ... told me the doctors were not willing I should speak with him. So I passed away, and never saw him more.*

While he lived, I wrote to Oliver Cromwell several times, and let him know that while he was persecuting God's people, they whom he accounted his enemies were preparing to come upon him. ...

Sometimes when we laid these sufferings before Oliver Cromwell, he would not believe it. Therefore Thomas Aldam and Anthony Pearson were moved to go through all the jails in England, and to get copies of Friends' commitments under the jailer's hands, that they might lay the weight of their sufferings

---

* This meeting of Fox with Cromwell is mentioned in Carlyle's *Oliver Cromwell*, Vol. IV., pp. 199, 200. Cromwell died on September 3, 1658.

upon Oliver Cromwell. And when he would not give order for the releasing of them, Thomas Aldam was moved to take his cap from off his head, and to rend it in pieces before him, and to say unto him, "So shall thy government be rent from thee and thy house."

From Kingston I went to . . . Buckinghamshire, where I had appointed a meeting, and the Lord's Truth and power were preciously manifested amongst us. After I had visited Friends in those parts, I returned to London, and soon after went into Essex, where I had not been long before I heard that the Protector was dead, and his son Richard made Protector. . . . Thereupon I came up to London again. . . . It was a time of great sufferings; for, besides imprisonments, through which many died, our meetings were greatly disturbed. They have thrown rotten eggs and wildfire into our meetings, and brought in drums beating and kettles to make noises with, that the Truth might not be heard. . . .

About this time great stirs were in the nation, the minds of people being unsettled. Much plotting and contriving there was by the several factions, to carry on their several interests. And a great care being upon me, lest any young or ignorant people, that might sometimes come amongst us, should be drawn into that snare, I was moved to give forth an epistle . . . warning . . . Friends to stay out of political plots.

Chapter Thirteen

In the First Year of King Charles
(1660)

W E PASSED THENCE to Tewkesbury and so to Worcester, visiting Friends in their meetings as we went. And in all my time I never saw such drunkenness as in the towns, for they had been choosing Parliament men. . . .

Passing into Derbyshire and Nottinghamshire, I came to Synderhill-Green, visiting Friends through all those parts in their meetings, and so on to Balby in Yorkshire, where our Yearly Meeting at that time was held in a great orchard of John Killam's, where it was supposed some thousands of people and Friends were gathered together.

In the morning I heard that a troop of horse was sent from York to break up our meeting, and that the militia, newly raised, was to join them. I went into the meeting, and stood up on a great stool, and after I had spoken some time two trumpeters came up, sounding their trumpets near me, and the captain of the troop cried, "Divide to the right and left, and make way." Then they rode up to me.

I was declaring the everlasting Truth and Word of life in the mighty power of the Lord. The captain bade me come down, for he was come to disperse our meeting. After some time I told him they all knew we were a peaceable people, and used to have such great meetings; but if he apprehended that we met in a hostile way, I desired him to make search among us, and if he found either sword or pistol about any there, let such suffer.

He told me he must see us dispersed, for he came all night on purpose to disperse us. I asked him what honor it would be to him to ride with swords and pistols amongst so many unarmed men and women as there were. If he would be still and quiet our meeting probably might not continue above two or three hours; and when it was done, as we came peaceably together, so we should part; for he might perceive the meeting was so large, that all the country thereabouts could not entertain them, but that they intended to depart towards their homes at night.

He said he could not stay to see the meeting ended, but must disperse them before he went. I desired him, then, if he himself could not stay, that he would let a dozen of his soldiers stay, and see the order and peaceableness of our meeting. He said he would permit us an hour's time, and left half a dozen soldiers with us. Then he went away with his troop, and Friends of the house gave the soldiers that stayed, and their horses, some food. . . .

When the captain was gone the soldiers that were left told us we might stay till night if we would. But we stayed but about three hours after, and had a glorious, powerful meeting; for the presence of the living God was manifest amongst us, and the Seed, Christ, was set over all. Friends were built upon Him, the foundation, and settled under His glorious, heavenly teaching.

After the meeting Friends passed away in peace, greatly refreshed with the presence of the Lord, and filled with joy and gladness that the Lord's power had given them such dominion. Many of the militia soldiers stayed also, much vexed that the captain and troopers had not broken up our meeting; and cursed the captain and his troopers. It was reported that they intended evil against us that day; but the troopers, instead of assisting them, were rather assistant to us, in not joining them as they expected, but preventing them from doing the mischief they designed. . . .

From Warmsworth I passed, in the Lord's power, to Barton Abbey, where I had a great meeting; thence to Thomas Taylor's; and so on to Skipton in Yorkshire, where was a general meeting of men Friends out of many counties concerning the affairs of the Church.

A Friend went naked shirtless through the town, declaring Truth, and was much beaten. Some other Friends also came to me all bloody. As I walked in the street, a desperate fellow had an intent to do me mischief; but he was prevented, and our meeting was quiet.

To this meeting came many Friends out of most parts of the nation; for it was about business relating to the Church both in this nation and beyond the seas. Several years before, when I was in the north, I was moved to recommend to Friends the setting up of this meeting for that . . . purpose for many Friends had suffered in diverse parts of the nation, their goods were taken from them contrary to law, and they understood not how to help themselves, or where to seek redress. But after this meeting was set up, several Friends who had been magistrates and others that understood something of the law, came thither, and were able to inform Friends, and to assist them in gathering up the sufferings, that they might be laid before the justices, judges, or Parliament.

This meeting had stood several years, and diverse justices and captains had come to break it up, but when they understood the business Friends met about, and saw their books and accounts of collections for relief of the poor, how we took care one county to help another, and to help our Friends beyond the seas, and provide for our poor, that none of them should be chargeable to their parishes, etc., the justices and officers confessed we did their work and passed away peaceably and lovingly, commending Friends' practice.

Sometimes there would come two hundred of the poor of other people, and wait there till the meeting was done (for all the country knew we met about the poor), and after the meeting Friends would send to the bakers for bread, and give every one of these poor people a loaf, how many so ever there were of them; for we were taught to "do good unto all; though especially to the household of faith. . . ."

I went next day to Swarthmore, Francis Howgill and Thomas Curtis being with me. I had not been long there before Henry Porter, a justice, sent a warrant by the chief constable and three petty constables to apprehend me. . . .

They kept me all night at the constable's house, and set a guard of fifteen or sixteen men to watch me; some of whom sat in the chimney, for fear I should go up it; such dark imaginations possessed them. . . .

Next morning, about six, I was putting on my boots and spurs to go with them before some justice; but they pulled off my spurs, took my knife out of my pocket, and hurried me away through the town, with a party of horse and abundance of people, not suffering me to stay till my own horse came down. . . .

Then they brought a little horse, and two of them took up one of my legs and put my foot in the stirrup, and two or three lifting over my other leg, set me upon it behind the saddle, and so led the horse by the halter; but I had nothing to hold by. When they were come some distance out of the town they beat the little horse, and made him kick and gallop. Thereupon I slipped off him. I told them they should not abuse the creature. They were much enraged at my getting off, and took me by the legs and feet, and set me upon the same horse, behind the saddle again. . . .

When I was come to Lancaster, the spirits of the people being mightily up, I stood and looked earnestly upon them, and they cried, "Look at his eyes!"* After awhile I spoke to them, and they were pretty sober. Then came a young man who took me to his house, and after a little time the officers took me to the house of Major Porter, the justice who had sent the warrant against me, and who had several others with him.

When I came in, I said, "Peace be amongst you." Porter asked me why I came into the country at that troublesome time.† I told him, "To visit my brethren." "But,"

---

* The power of Fox's gaze was often noted.

† With the Cromwell regime fallen and the Stuarts restarted, any travel or meeting was suspect.

said he, "you have great meetings up and down." I told him that though we had, our meetings were known throughout the nation to be peaceable, and we were a peaceable people.

He said that we saw the devil in people's faces. I told him that if I saw a drunkard, or a swearer, or a peevish heady man, I could not say I saw the Spirit of God in him. . . .

He said we could express ourselves well enough, and he would not dispute with me; but he would restrain me. I desired to know for what, and by whose order he had sent his warrant for me; and I complained to him of the abuse of the constables and other officers after they had taken me, and in their bringing me thither. He would not take notice of that, but told me he had an order, but would not let me see it; . . . and besides, "A prisoner," he said, "is not to see for what he is committed." I told him that was not reason; for how, then, should he make his defense? I said I ought to have a copy of it. . . .

Then he called to his clerk, saying, "Is it not ready yet? Bring it"; meaning the mittimus containing the charge. But it not being ready, he told me I was a disturber of the nation. I told him I had been a blessing to the nation, in and through the Lord's power and Truth; and that the Spirit of God in all consciences would answer it. Then he charged me as an enemy to the King, that I endeavored to raise a new war, and imbrue the nation in blood again. I told him I had never learned the postures of war, but was clear and innocent as a child concerning those things. . . .

Then came the clerk with the mittimus, and the jailer was sent for and commanded to take me, put me into the Dark-house, and let none come at me, but to keep me there close prisoner till I should be delivered by the King or Parliament. Then the justice asked the constables where my horse was. "For I hear," said he, "he hath a good horse; have ye brought his horse? . . ."

When I finally had . . . got the heads of the charge contained in the mittimus, I wrote a plain answer in vindication of my innocency in each particular; as follows:

> I am a prisoner at Lancaster, committed by Justice Porter. A copy of the mittimus I cannot get, but such expressions I am told are in it as are very untrue; as that I am generally suspected to be a common disturber of the nation's peace, an enemy to the King, and that I, with others, endeavor to raise insurrections to embroil the nation in blood; all of which is utterly false, and I do, in every part thereof, deny it.

> For I am not a person generally suspected to be a disturber of the nation's peace, nor have I given any cause for such suspicion; for through the nation I have been tried for these things formerly. In the days of

Oliver I was taken up on pretense of raising arms against him, which was also false; for I meddled not with raising arms at all. Yet I was then carried up a prisoner to London, and brought before him; when I cleared myself, and denied the drawing of a carnal weapon against him, or any man upon the earth; for my weapons are spiritual, which take away the occasion of war, and lead into peace. Upon my declaring this to Oliver, I was set at liberty by him.

After this I was taken and sent to prison by Major Ceely in Cornwall, who, when I was brought before the judge, informed against me that I took him aside, and told him that I could raise forty thousand men in an hour's time, to involve the nation in blood, and bring in King Charles. This also was utterly false, and a lie of his own inventing as was then proved upon him for I never spoke any such word to him.

I never was found in any plot; I never took any engagement or oath; nor have I ever learned war postures. As those were false charges against me then, so are these now which come from Major Porter, who is lately appointed to be justice, but formerly wanted power to exercise his cruelty against us; which is but the wickedness of the old enemy. The peace of the nation I am not a disturber of, nor ever was; but I seek the peace of it, and of all men, and stand for all nations' peace, and all men's peace upon the earth, and wish all knew my innocency in these things.

And whereas Major Porter saith I am an enemy to the King, this is false; for my love is to him and to all men, even though they be enemies to God, to themselves, and to me. And I can say it is of the Lord that the King is come in, to bring down many unrighteously set up; of which I had a sight three years before he came in. It is much Major Porter should say I am an enemy to the King; for I have no reason so to be, he having done nothing against me.

But I have been often imprisoned and persecuted these eleven or twelve years by those that have been both against the King and his father, even the party by whom Porter was made a major and for whom he bore arms;* but not by them

---

* Porter had previously been on the other side.

that were for the King. I was never an enemy to the King, nor to any man's person upon the earth. I am in the love that fulfils the law, which thinks no evil, but loves even enemies; and would have the King saved, and come to the knowledge of the Truth, and be brought into the fear of the Lord, to receive His wisdom from above, by which all things were made and created; that with that wisdom he may order all things to the glory of God.

Whereas he calleth me "A chief upholder of the Quakers' sect," I answer: The Quakers are not a sect, but are in the power of God, which was before sects were, and witness the election before the world began, and are come to live in the life in which the prophets and apostles lived, who gave forth the Scriptures; therefore are we hated by envious, wrathful, wicked, persecuting men. But God is the upholder of us all by His mighty power, and preserves us from the wrath of the wicked that would swallow us up.

And whereas he saith that I, together with others of my fanatic opinion, as he calls it, have of late endeavored to raise insurrections, and to embroil the whole kingdom in blood, I answer, This is altogether false. To these things I am as a child; I know nothing of them. The postures of war I never learned; my weapons are spiritual and not carnal, for with carnal weapons I do not fight. I am a follower of Him who said, "My kingdom is not of this world," and though these lies and slanders are raised upon me, I deny drawing any carnal weapon against the King or Parliament, or any man upon the earth. For I am come to the end of the Law, but am in that which saves men's lives. A witness I am against all murderers, plotters, and all such as would imbrue the nation in blood; for it is not in my heart to have any man's life destroyed.

And as for the word fanatic, which signifies furious, foolish, mad, etc., he might have considered himself before he had used that word, and have learned the humility which goes before honor. We are not furious, foolish, or mad; but through patience and meekness have borne lies, slanders and persecutions many years, and have undergone great sufferings. The spiritual man, that wrestles not with flesh and blood, and the Spirit that reproves sin in the gate, which is the Spirit of Truth, wisdom, and sound judgment, is not mad, foolish, furious, which fanatic signifies; but all are of a mad, furious, foolish spirit that in their furiousness, foolishness and rage wrestle with flesh and blood, with carnal weapons. This is not the Spirit of God, but of error, that persecutes in a mad, blind zeal, like Nebuchadnezzar and Saul.

Inasmuch as I am ordered to be kept prisoner till I be delivered by order from the King or Parliament, therefore I have written these things to be laid before you, the King and Parliament, that ye may consider of them before ye act anything therein; that ye may weigh, in the wisdom of God, the intent and end of men's spirits, lest ye act the thing that will bring the hand of the Lord upon you and against you, as many who have been in authority have done before you, whom God hath overthrown. In Him we trust whom we fear and cry unto day and night, who hath heard us, doth hear us, and will hear us, and avenge our cause. Much innocent blood hath been shed. Many have been persecuted to death by such as were in authority before you, whom God hath vomited out because they turned against the just. Therefore consider

your standing now that ye have the day, and
receive this as a warning of love to you."

From an innocent sufferer in bonds, and
close prisoner in Lancaster Castle, called

George Fox

After this Margaret Fell determined to go to
London,* to speak with the King about my being
taken, and to show him the manner of it, and the
unjust dealing and evil usage I had received. When
Justice Porter heard of this, he vapored that he would
go and meet her in the gap. But when he came before
the King, having been a zealous man for the Parliament against the King, several of the courtiers spoke
to him concerning his plundering their houses; so
that he quickly had enough of the court, and soon
returned into the country.

Meanwhile the jailer seemed very fearful, and said
he was afraid Major Porter would hang him because
he had not put me in the Dark-house. But when the
jailer waited on him after his return from London, he
was very blank and down, and asked how I did, pretending he would find a way to set me at liberty. But
having overshot himself in his mittimus by ordering
me "to be kept a prisoner till I should be delivered

---

* Judge Fell had died in 1658.

by the King or Parliament," he had put it out of his power to release me if he would.

He was the more down also upon reading a letter which I sent him; for when he was in the height of his rage and threats against me, and thought to ingratiate himself into the King's favor by imprisoning me, I was moved to write to him and put him in mind how fierce he had been against the King and his party, though now he would wish to be thought zealous for the King. . . .

Meanwhile I wrote:

TO THE KING

King Charles:

Thou camest not into this nation by sword, nor by victory of war, but by the power of the Lord. Now, if thou dost not live in this power, thou wilt not prosper.

. . . If thou dost not stop persecution and persecutors, and take away all laws that hold up persecution about religion; if thou persist in them, and uphold persecution, that will make thee as blind as those that have gone before thee: for persecution hath always blinded those that have gone into it. Such God by his power overthrows, doeth His valiant acts upon, and bringeth salvation to His oppressed ones.

If thou bear the sword in vain, and let drunkenness, oaths, plays, May-games, as setting up of May-poles, with the image of the crown atop of them, with such like abominations and vanities, be encouraged or go unpunished, the nation will quickly turn like Sodom and Gomorrah, and be as bad as those men of the old world, who grieved the Lord till He overthrew them. So He will overthrow you if these things be not suppressed.*

Hardly ever before has there been so much wickedness at liberty as there is at this day, as though there were no terror nor sword of magistracy. Such looseness doth not grace a government, nor please them that do well. Our prayers are for them that are in authority, that under them we may live a godly life in peace, and that we may not be brought into ungodliness by them. Hear and consider, and do good in thy time, whilst thou hast power; be merciful and forgive; that is the way to overcome and obtain the kingdom of Christ.

G. F.

---

* Many things forbidden by the Puritans, such as plays, came back under Charles II. Fox does not approve of some of these things, as outlined.

. . . Eventually the sheriff would yield to remove me to London, . . . but only if I would . . . bear the charges; which I . . . refused to do. . . .

When they considered what a charge it would be to them to send up a party of horse with me, they altered their purpose, and concluded to send me up guarded only by the jailer and some bailiffs. But upon farther consideration they found that this also would be a great charge to them, and therefore they sent for me to the jailer's house, and told me that if I would post bail and promise . . . that I would be in London on such a day of the term, I should have leave to go up with some of my own friends.

I told them I would neither put in bail, nor give one piece of silver to the jailer; for I was an innocent man—that they had imprisoned me wrongfully, and laid a false charge upon me. Nevertheless, I said, if they would let me go up with one or two of my friends to bear me company, I might go up and be in London on such a day, if the Lord should permit; and if they desired it, I or any of my friends that went with me would carry up their charge against myself.

When they saw they could do no otherwise with me, the sheriff consented that I should come up with some of my friends, without any other engagement than my word, to appear before the judges at London such a day of the term, if the Lord should permit. . . .

When we came to Charing-Cross in London, multitudes of people were gathered together to see the burning of the bowels of some of Cromwell's ... judges, who had been hanged, drawn and quartered. ...

... When we had delivered to the judges the charge that was against me, and they had read to those words, "that I and my friends were embroiling the nation in blood," etc., they struck their hands on the table. Whereupon I told them that I was the man whom that charge was against, but I was as innocent of any such thing as a newborn child, and had brought it up myself; and some of my friends came up with me, without any guard.

As yet they had not minded my hat, but now seeing it on, they said, "What, do you stand with your hat on!" I told them I did not so in any contempt of them. Then they commanded it to be taken off; and when they called for the marshal of the King's Bench, they said to him, "You must take this man and secure him; but let him have a chamber, and not be put amongst the prisoners."

"My lord," said the marshal, "I have no chamber to put him into; my house is so full I cannot tell where to provide a room for him but amongst the prisoners."

"Nay," said the judge, "you must not put him amongst the prisoners."

But when the marshal still answered that he had no other place wherein to put me, Judge Foster said to me, "Will you appear tomorrow about ten o'clock at the King's Bench bar in Westminster Hall?"

I said, "Yes, if the Lord gives me strength."

Then said Judge Foster to the other judge, "If he says Yes, and promises it, you may take his word;" so I was dismissed.

Next day I appeared at the King's Bench bar at the hour appointed. . . .

The charge against me was read openly. The people were moderate, and the judges cool and loving; and the Lord's mercy was to them. But when they came to that part which said that I and my friends were embroiling the nation in blood, and raising a new war, and that I was an enemy to the King, etc., they lifted up their hands.

Then, stretching out my arms, I said, "I am the man whom that charge is against; but I am as innocent as a child concerning the charge, and have never learned any war postures. And," said I, "do ye think that, if I and my friends had been such men as the charge declares, I would have brought it up myself against myself? Or that I should have been suffered to come up with only one or two of my friends with me? Had I been such a man as this charge sets forth, I had need to be guarded with a troop or two of horse. But the sheriff and magistrates of Lancashire thought fit to let me and my friends come up with it ourselves, nearly two hundred miles, without any guard at all; which, ye may be sure, they would not have done, had they looked upon me to be such a man. . . ."

. . . Then stood up Esquire Marsh, who was of the King's bedchamber, and told the judges it was the King's pleasure that I should be set at liberty, seeing no accuser came up against me. . . .

Thus, after I had been a prisoner somewhat more than twenty weeks, I was freely set at liberty by the King's command, the Lord's power having wonderfully wrought for the clearing of my innocency, and Porter, who committed me, not daring to appear to make good the charge he had falsely suggested against me. But, after it was known I was discharged, a company of envious, wicked spirits were troubled, and terror took hold of Justice Porter; for he was afraid I would take the advantage of the law against him for my wrong imprisonment, and thereby undo him, his wife, and children. And indeed I was pressed by some in authority to make him and the rest examples; but I said I should leave them to the Lord; if the Lord forgave them I should not trouble myself with them.

Chapter Fourteen

Labors, Dangers, and Sufferings

(1661–1662)

SOME FRIENDS WERE . . . brought into the House of Lords, to declare . . . the reasons why they could not pay tithes for church support, swear, go to the steeple-house worship, or join with others in worship; and the Lords heard them moderately. There being about seven hundred Friends in prison, who had been committed under Oliver's and Richard's government, . . . when the King came in, he set them all at liberty.

There seemed at that time an inclination and intention in the government to grant Friends liberty, because those in authority were sensible that we had suffered as well as they under the former powers. But still, when anything was going forward in order thereto, some dirty spirits or other, that would seem to be for us, threw something in the way to stop it. It was said there was an instrument drawn up for confirming our liberty, and that it only wanted signing; when suddenly that wicked attempt of the Fifth-monarchy people* broke out, and put the city and nation in an uproar. . . .

Great rifling of houses there was at this time to search for people. I went to a private Friend's house, and Richard Hubberthorn was with me. There we drew up a declaration against plots and fightings, to be presented to the King and Council; . . . when finished, and sent to print, it was taken in the press.

On this insurrection of the Fifth Monarchy Men, great havoc . . . resulted both in city and country, so that it was dangerous for sober people to stir abroad for several weeks after. Men or women could hardly go up and down the streets to buy provisions for their families without being abused. . . .

The prisons were now everywhere filled with Friends and others, in the city and country, and the posts were so laid for the searching of letters that

---

* The insurrection of Fifth Monarchy Men, who triggered a new persecution of Friends.

none could pass unsearched. We heard of several thousands of our Friends that were cast into prison in several parts of the nation, and Margaret Fell carried an account of them to the King and Council. The next week we had a further account of several thousands more that were cast into prison, and she went and laid them also before the King and Council. They wondered how we could have such intelligence, seeing they had given such strict charge for the intercepting of all letters; but the Lord did so order it that we had an account notwithstanding all their stoppings.

Soon after the King gave forth a proclamation that no soldiers should search any house without a constable. But the jails were still full, many thousands of Friends being in prison; which mischief was occasioned by the wicked rising of the Fifth Monarchy Men. But when those that were taken came to be executed, they did us the justice to clear us openly from having any hand in or knowledge of their plot.

After that, the King being continually importuned thereunto issued a declaration that Friends should be set at liberty without paying fees. But great labor, travail, and pains were taken before this was obtained; for Thomas Moore and Margaret Fell went often to the King about it.

Much blood was shed this year, many of . . . Cromwell's judges being hung, drawn and quartered. Amongst them that so suffered, Colonel Hacker was one. He had sent me prisoner from Leicester to London in Oliver's time, of which an account is given before. A sad day it was and a repaying of blood with blood. For in the time of Oliver Cromwell, when several men were put to death by him, being hung, drawn, and quartered for pretended treasons, I felt from the Lord God that their blood would be required; and I said as much then to several.

And now, upon the King's return, several that had been against him were put to death, as the others that were for him had been before by Oliver. This was sad work, destroying people; contrary to the nature of Christians, who have the nature of lambs and sheep. But there was a secret hand in bringing this day upon that hypocritical generation of professors, who, being got into power, grew proud, haughty, and cruel beyond others, and persecuted the people of God without pity. . . .

For that for which we suffered, and for which our goods were spoiled, was our obedience to the Lord in His Power and His Spirit. He was able to help and to succor, and we had no helper in the earth but Him. And He heard the cries of His people, and brought an overflowing scourge over the heads of all our persecutors, which brought a dread and a fear amongst and on them all. So that those who had nicknamed us (who are the children of Light) and in scorn called us Quakers, the Lord made to quake; and many of them would have been glad to hide themselves amongst us; and some of them, through the distress that came upon them, did at length come to confess to the Truth.

Many ways were these professors warned, by word, by writing, and by signs; but they would believe none till it was too late. William Sympson was moved of the Lord to go at several times for three years naked, shirtless, and barefooted before them, as a sign to them, in markets, courts, towns, cities, to priests' houses, and to great men's houses, telling them, "So shall ye be stripped naked as I am stripped naked!" And sometimes he was moved to put on hair-sack-cloth, and to besmear his face, and to tell them, "So will the Lord God besmear all your religion as I am besmeared."

Great sufferings did that poor man undergo, sore whippings with horse whips and coach whips on his bare body, grievous stoning and imprisonments, in three years' time, before the King came in, that they might have taken warning; but they would not, and rewarded his love with cruel usage. Only the mayor of Cambridge did nobly to him, for he put his gown about him and took him into his house.

Another Friend, Robert Huntingdon, was moved of the Lord to go into Carlisle steeple-house with . . . a halter about his neck to show them that a halter was coming upon them; which was fulfilled upon some of our persecutors not long after. . . .

After this, on a lecture day, Richard Sale was moved to go to the steeple-house in the time of their worship, and to carry those persecuting priests and people a lantern and candle, as a figure of their darkness. But they cruelly abused him, and like dark professors as they were put him into their prison called Little Ease,* and so squeezed his body therein that not long after he died. ...

About this time we had an account that John Love, a Friend that was moved to go and bear testimony against the idolatry of the Papists, was dead in prison at Rome; it was suspected he was privately put to death. Also before this time we received account from New England that the government there had made a law to banish the Quakers out of their colonies, upon pain of death in case they returned; that several of our Friends, having been so banished and returning, were thereupon taken and actually hanged, and that diverse more were in prison, in danger of the like sentence being executed upon them. When those were put to death I was in prison at Lancaster, and had a perfect sense of their sufferings as though it had been myself, and as though the halter had been put about my own neck, though we had not at that time heard of it.

As soon as we heard of it, Edward Burrough went to the King and told him that there was a vein of

---

* A tight hole, 17" wide, cut out of rock with an even tighter door, and only 4' 6" high. Pushing in a prisoner was a form of torture that killed Sale, a fairly big man.

innocent blood opened in his dominions which, if it were not stopped, would overrun all. To this the King replied, ". . . I will stop that vein." Edward Burrough said, "Then do it speedily for we know not how many may soon be put to death." The King answered, "As speedily as ye will. Call," (said he to some present) "the secretary and I will do it presently."

The secretary being called, a mandamus was forthwith granted. A day or two after, Edward Burrough going again to the King to desire the matter might be expedited, the King said he had no occasion at present to send a ship thither, but if we would send one we might do it as soon as we would. Edward then asked the King if it would please him to grant his deputation to one called a Quaker to carry the mandamus to New England. He said, "Yes, to whom ye will. . . ."

The townsmen at Boston, seeing a ship come into the bay with English colors, soon came on board and asked for the captain. Ralph Goldsmith told them he was the commander. They asked him if he had any letters. He said, "Yes." They asked if he would deliver them. He said, "No; not today."

So they went ashore and reported that there was a ship full of Quakers, and that Samuel Shattuck, who they knew was by their law to be put to death if he came again after banishment, was among them, but they knew not his errand nor his authority.

So all were kept close that day, and none of the ship's company suffered to go on shore. Next morning Samuel Shattuck, the King's deputy, and Ralph Goldsmith, went on shore, and, sending back to the ship the men that landed them, they two went through the town to Governor John Endicott's door, and knocked. He sent out a man to know their business. They sent him word that their business was from the King of England, and that they would deliver their message to no one but the Governor himself.

Thereupon they were admitted, and the Governor came to them; and having received the deputation and the mandamus, he put off his hat and looked upon them. Then, going out, he bade the Friends follow him. He went to the deputy governor, and after a short consultation came out to the Friends, and said, "We shall obey his majesty's commands."

After this the master gave liberty to the passengers to come on shore, and presently the noise of the business flew about the town; and the Friends of the town and the passengers of the ship met together to offer up their praises and thanksgivings to God, who had so wonderfully delivered them from the teeth of the devourer.

While they were thus met, in came a poor Friend, who, being sentenced by their bloody law to die, had lain some time in irons expecting execution. This added to their joy, and caused them to lift up their hearts in high praise to God, who is worthy forever to have the praise, the glory, and the honor; for He only is able to deliver, to save, and support all that sincerely put their trust in Him. . . .

I went also to Governor Winthrop, and discoursed with him on these matters. He assured me that he had no hand in putting our Friends to death or in any way persecuting them; but was one of them that protested against it. . . .

Before this, while I was prisoner in Lancaster Castle, the book called the "Battledore" was published, which was written to show that in all languages Thou and Thee is the proper and usual form of speech to a single person; and You to more than one. This was set forth in examples or instances taken from the Scriptures, and books of teaching, in about thirty languages. J. Stubbs and Benjamin Furly took great pains in compiling it, which I set them upon; and some things I added to it.

When it was finished, copies were presented to the King and his Council, to the Bishops of Canterbury and London, and to the two universities one each; and many purchased them. The King said it was the proper language of all nations; and the Bishop of Canterbury, being asked what he thought of it, was at a stand, and could not tell what to say to it. For it did so inform and convince people, that few afterwards were so rugged toward us for saying Thou and Thee to a single person, whereas . . . before they were exceedingly fierce against us.

Thou and Thee was a sore cut to proud flesh, and them that sought self-honor, who, though they would say it to God and Christ, could not endure to have it said to themselves. So that we were often beaten and abused, and sometimes in danger of our lives, for using those words to some proud men, who would say, "What! You ill-bred clown, do you Thou me?" as though Christian breeding consisted in saying You to one; which is contrary to all their grammars and teaching books, by which they instructed their youth.*

About this time many Papists and Jesuits began to fawn upon Friends, and talked up and down where they came, that of all the sects the Quakers were the best and most self-denying people; and . . . said it was great pity that they did not return to the Holy Mother Church. . . .

But when I understood it, I said to Friends, "Let us discourse with them, be they what they will." So a time being appointed at Gerrard Roberts's, there came two of them like courtiers. . . .

I asked them the same question that I had formerly asked a Jesuit, namely, whether the Church of Rome was not degenerated from the Church in the primitive times, from the Spirit, power, and practice that they

---

* Thou was the familiar form. You was, in addition to being the plural form, also a term of respect. Hence a young person would be expected to say you, not thou, to an elder, and self-important people would not want anyone to "thou" them. Although "you" was a term of respect, God was "thou," because we were seen as his children and on intimate terms with Him.

had in in the Apostles' times? He to whom I put this question, being subtle, said he would not answer it. I asked him why. But he would show no reason. His companion said he would answer me; and said that they were not degenerated from the Church in the primitive times. I asked the other whether he was of the same mind. He said, "Yes."

Then I replied that, for the better understanding one of another, and that there might be no mistake, I would repeat my question over again after this manner: "Is the Church of Rome now in the same purity, practice, power, and Spirit that the Church in the Apostles' time was in?" When they saw we would be exact with them, they flew off and denied that, saying it was presumption in any to say they had the same power and Spirit which the Apostles had. . . .

Then I began to tell them how that evil spirit by which they were led had led them to pray by beads and to images, and to set up nunneries, friaries, and monasteries, and to put people to death for religion; which practices I showed them were below the law, and far short of the gospel, in which is liberty.

They were soon weary of this discourse, and went their way, and gave a charge, as we heard, to the Papists, that they should not dispute with us, nor read any of our books.

So we were rid of them; but we had reasonings with all the other sects, Presbyterians, Independents, Seekers,

Baptists, Episcopal men, Socinians, Brownists, Lutherans, Calvinists, Arminians, Fifth Monarchy Men, Familists, Muggletonians, and Ranters; none of which would affirm that they had the same power and Spirit that the Apostles had and were in; so in that power and Spirit the Lord gave us dominion over them all.

As for the Fifth Monarchy Men I was moved to give forth a paper, to manifest their error to them; for they looked for Christ's personal coming in an outward form and manner, and fixed the time to the year 1666; at which time some of them prepared themselves when it thundered and rained, thinking Christ was then come to set up His kingdom. . . .

And I told them that when Christ was on earth, He said His kingdom was not of this world; if it had been, His servants would have fought; but it was not, therefore His servants did not fight. Therefore all the Fifth Monarchy Men that are fighters with carnal weapons are none of Christ's servants, but the beast's and the whore's. Christ said, "All power in heaven and in earth is given to me"; so then His kingdom was set up above sixteen hundred years ago, and He reigns. "And we see Jesus Christ reign," said the Apostle, "and He shall reign till all things be put under His feet"; though all things are not yet put under His feet, nor subdued.

This year several Friends were moved to go beyond the seas, to publish Truth in foreign countries. John

Stubbs, and Henry Fell, and Richard Costrop were moved to go towards China and Prester John's country;* but no masters of ships would carry them. With much ado they got a warrant from the King; but the East India Company found ways to thwart . . . it, and the masters of their ships would not carry them.

Then they went into Holland, hoping to get passage there, but none could they get there either. Then John Stubbs and Henry Fell took shipping for Alexandria, in Egypt, intending to go thence by the caravans. . . .

John Stubbs and Henry Fell reached Alexandria; but they had not been long there before the English consul banished them; yet before they came away, they dispersed many books and papers for opening the principles and way of Truth to the Turks and Grecians. They gave the book called, "The Pope's Strength Broken," to an old friar, for him to give or send to the Pope. When the friar had perused it he placed his hand on his breast and confessed, "What is written therein is truth; but," said he, "if I should confess it openly, they would burn me."

John Stubbs and Henry Fell, not being suffered to go further, returned to England, and came to London again. John had a vision that the English and Dutch, who had joined together not to carry them, would fall out one with the other; and so it came to pass.

---

* A legendary Christian realm in Africa often identified with Ethiopia.

Among the exercises and troubles that Friends had from without, one was concerning Friends' marriages, which sometimes were called in question.* In this year there happened to be a trial ... at the assize at Nottingham concerning a Friend's marriage.

The case was thus: Some years before two Friends were joined together in marriage amongst Friends, and lived together as man and wife about two years. Then the man died, leaving his wife with child, and leaving an estate in lands of copyhold. When the woman was delivered, the jury presented the child heir to its father's lands, and accordingly the child was admitted; afterwards another Friend married the widow. After that a person near of kin to her former husband brought his action against the Friend who had last married her, endeavoring to dispossess them, and deprive the child of the inheritance, and to possess himself thereof as next heir to the woman's first husband. To effect this he endeavored to prove the child illegitimate, alleging that the marriage was not according to law. . . .

. . . After the counsel on both sides had pleaded before the Judge (viz., Judge Archer) took the matter in hand, and opened it to them, telling them, "There was a marriage in paradise when Adam took Eve and Eve took Adam, and it was the consent of the parties

---

* Because they were married without clergyman or magistrate. The ceremony takes the form of a mutual vow, taken when Friends have gathered.

that made a marriage." And for the Quakers, he said, he did not know their opinions; but he did not believe they went together as brute beasts, as had been said of them, but as Christians; and therefore he did believe the marriage was lawful, and the child lawful heir. . . .

Now, there being very many Friends in prison in the nation, Richard Hubberthorn and I drew up a paper concerning them, and got it delivered to the King, that he might understand how we were dealt with by his officers. It was directed thus:

> For the King:
>
> Friend,
>
> Who art the chief ruler of these dominions, here is a list of some of the sufferings of the people of God, in scorn called Quakers, that have suffered under the changeable powers before thee, by whom there have been imprisoned, and under whom there have suffered for good conscience's sake, and for bearing testimony to the truth as it is in Jesus, three thousand one hundred and seventy-three persons; and there lie yet in prison, in the name of the Commonwealth, seventy-three persons that we know of. And there died in prison in the time of the Commonwealth, and of Oliver and Richard the

Protectors, through cruel and hard imprisonments, upon nasty straw and in dungeons, thirty-two persons. There have been also imprisoned in thy name, since thy arrival, by such as thought to ingratiate themselves thereby with thee, three thousand sixty and eight persons. Besides this our meetings are daily broken up by men with clubs and arms, though we meet peaceably, according to the practice of God's people in the primitive times, and our Friends are thrown into waters, and trodden upon, till the very blood gushes out of them; the number of which abuses can hardly be uttered.

Now this we would have of thee, to set them at liberty that lie in prison in the names of the Commonwealth, and of the two Protectors, and them that lie in thy own name, for speaking the truth, and for good conscience's sake, who have not lifted up a hand against thee or any man; and that the meetings of our Friends, who meet peaceably together in the fear of God, to worship Him, may not be broken up by rude people with their clubs, swords, and staves. . . .

Chapter Fifteen

In Prison for Not Swearing
(1662–1665)

A FTER I HAD made some stay in London, …
I went into the country, having with me
Alexander Parker and John Stubbs. We
traveled through the Country, visiting Friends' meetings, till we came to Bristol. . . .

From Barnet Hills we came to Swannington, in
Leicestershire, where William Smith and some other
Friends visited me; but they went away towards
nights leaving me at a Friend's house in Swannington.

At night, as I was sitting in the hall speaking to a
widow woman and her daughter, Lord Beaumont

came with a company of soldiers, who, slapping their swords on the door, rushed into the house with swords and pistols in their hands, crying, "Put out the candles and make fast the doors." Then they seized upon the Friends in the house. . . .

. . . The constable set a watch of the townspeople upon us that night, and had us next morning to his house, about a mile from Swannington.

When we came before him, he told us that we had met "contrary to the Act. . . ."* Then he asked whether we would take the oaths of allegiance and supremacy. I told him I never took any oath in my life. . . . Yet still he would force the oath upon us. I desired him to show us the oath, that we might see whether we were the persons it was to be tendered to, and whether it was not for the discovery of popish recusants. . . .

When the sessions came we were brought before the justices, with many more Friends, sent to prison whilst we were there, to the number of about twenty. The jailer put us into the place where the thieves were put, and then some of the justices began to tender the oaths of allegiance and supremacy† to us. I told them

---

* An act passed in 1662 "for preventing mischiefs and dangers that may arise by certain persons called Quakers, and others refusing to take oaths." The act forbade more than five "Quakers to assemble in any place under pretense of joining in a religious worship not authorized by the laws of this realm."

† The Act of Supremacy made the British sovereign head of the Church.

I never took any oath in my life; and they knew we could not swear, because Christ and His Apostle forbade it; therefore they but put it as a snare to us. We told them that if they could prove that, after Christ and the Apostle had forbidden swearing, they did ever command Christians to swear, then we would take these oaths; otherwise we were resolved to obey Christ's command and the Apostle's exhortation.

They said we must take the oath that we might manifest our allegiance to the King. I told them I had been formerly sent up a prisoner by Colonel Hacker, from that town to London, under pretense that I had held meetings to plot to bring in King Charles. I also desired them to read our mittimus, which set forth the cause of our commitment to be that we "were to have a meeting"; and I said Lord Beaumont could not by that act send us to jail unless we had been taken at a meeting, and found to be such persons as the act speaks of; therefore we desired that they would read the mittimus and see how wrongfully we were imprisoned.

They would not take notice of the mittimus, but called a jury and indicted us for refusing to take the oaths of allegiance and supremacy. . . .

While we were standing where the thieves . . . stood, a cut-purse had his hand in several Friends' pockets. Friends declared it to the justices, and showed them the man. They called him up before them, and upon examination he could not deny it; yet they set him at liberty.

It was not long before the jury returned, and brought us in guilty; and after some words, the justices whispered together, and bid the jailer take us to prison again; but the Lord's power was over them, and His everlasting Truth, which we declared boldly amongst them. There being a great concourse of people, most of them followed us; so that the crier and bailiffs were fain to call the people back again to the court.

We declared the Truth as we went along the streets, till we came to the jail, the streets being full of people.

When we were in our chamber again, after some time the jailer came to us and desired all to go forth that were not prisoners. When they were gone he said, "Gentlemen, it is the court's pleasure that ye should be set at liberty, except those that are in for tithes; and you know there are fees due to me; but I shall leave it to you to give me what you will."

Thus we were all set at liberty on a sudden, and passed every one into our services. Leonard Fell went with me again to Swannington.

I had a letter from Lord Hastings, who, hearing of my imprisonment, had written from London to the justices of the sessions to set me at liberty. I had not delivered this letter to the justices; whether any knowledge of his mind received through another hand made them discharge us so suddenly, I know not. This letter I carried to Lord Beaumont, who had sent us to prison. When he had broken it open and read it, he seemed much troubled; but at last he came a little lower, yet threatened us that if we had any more meetings at Swannington, he would break them up and send us to prison again.

But, notwithstanding his threats, we went to Swannington, and had a meeting with Friends there, and he neither came nor sent to break it up.

. . . Then I went to London, . . . into Essex, and so to Norfolk, having great meetings. . . . I came over the sands to Swarthmore. There they told me that Colonel Kirby had sent his lieutenant, who had searched trunks and chests for me. . . .

Next day an officer came with his sword and pistols to take me. I told him I knew his errand before, and had given myself to be taken; for if I would have escaped their imprisonment I could have been forty miles off before he came; but I was an innocent man, and so it mattered not what they could do to me. He asked me how I heard of it, seeing the order was made privately in a parlor. I said it was no matter for that; it was sufficient that I heard it.

I asked him to let me see his order, whereupon he laid his hand on his sword, and said I must go with him before the lieutenant to answer such questions as they should propound to me. I told him it was but civil and reasonable for him to let me see his order; but he would not. Then said I, "I am ready."

So I went along with him, and Margaret Fell accompanied us to Houlker Stall. When we came thither there was one Rawlinson, a justice, and one called Sir George Middleton, and many more that I did not know, besides old Justice Preston, who lived there. . . .

Then said George Middleton, "You deny God, and the Church, and the faith."

I replied, "Nay, I own God and the true Church, and the true faith. But what Church dost thou own?" said I (for I understood he was a Papist).

Then he turned again and said, "You are a rebel and a traitor."

I asked him to whom he spoke, or whom did he call rebel. He was so full of envy that for awhile he could not speak, but at last he said, "I spoke it to you."

With that I struck my hand on the table, and told him, "I have suffered more than twenty such as thou; more than any that is here; for I have been cast into Derby dungeon for six months together, and have suffered much because I would not take up arms against this King before Worcester fight. I was sent up a prisoner out of my own country by Colonel Hacker to Oliver Cromwell, as a plotter to bring in King Charles in the year 1654. I have nothing but love and goodwill to the King, and desire the eternal good and welfare of him and all his subjects."

"Did you ever hear the like?" said Middleton. "Nay," said I. "Ye may hear it again if ye will. For ye talk of the King, a company of you, but where were ye in Oliver's days, and what did ye do then for him? But I have more love to the King for his eternal good and welfare than any of you have. . . ."

Then George Middleton cried, "Bring the book, and put the oaths of allegiance and supremacy to him."

Now he himself being a Papist, I asked him whether he, who was a swearer, had taken the oath of supremacy.* As for us, we could not swear at all, because Christ and the Apostle had forbidden it.

Some of them would not have had the oath put to me, but would have set me at liberty. The rest would not agree to it, for this was their last snare, and they had no other way to get me into prison. . . . †

So they tendered me the oath, which I could not take; whereupon they were about to make my mittimus to send me to Lancaster jail; but considering of it, they only engaged me to appear at the sessions, and for that time dismissed me. . . .

The sessions coming on, I went to Lancaster, and appeared according to my engagement. There was upon the bench Justice Fleming, who had bid five pounds in Westmoreland to any man that would

---

* The oath of supremacy, putting the British king in charge of the Church, was difficult for a Catholic to sign. Sir Thomas More was beheaded by Henry VIII precisely for refusing to swear to this Act.

† Refusal to swear in general was the usual charge against Friends during the reign of Charles II.

apprehend me, for he was a justice both in Westmoreland and Lancashire. There were also Justice Spencer, Colonel West, and old Justice Rawlinson, the lawyer, who gave the charge, and was very sharp against Truth and Friends. . . .

Then Rawlinson asked me whether I held it was unlawful to swear. This question he put on purpose to ensnare me; for by the recent . . . Act . . . those . . . were liable to banishment or a great fine who . . . should say it was unlawful to swear. But I, seeing the snare, avoided it, and told him that "in the time of the law amongst the Jews, before Christ came, the law commanded them to swear; but Christ, who doth fulfill the law in His gospel time, commands not to swear at all; and the apostle James forbids swearing, even to them that were Jews, and had the law of God."

After much discourse, they called for the jailer, and committed me to prison. . . .

Several other Friends were committed to prison, some for meeting to worship God, and some for not swearing; so that the prison was very full. . . .

Several who were imprisoned on that account were known to be men that had served the King in his wars, and had hazarded their lives in the field in his cause, and had suffered great hardships, with the loss of much blood, for him, and had always stood faithful to him from first to last, and had never received any pay for their service. To be thus requited for all their faithful services and sufferings, and that by them who . . . pretended to be the King's friends, was hard, unkind, and ungrateful dealing.

At length the justices, being continually attended with complaints of grievances, released some of the Friends, but kept diverse of them still in prison.

I was kept till the assize, and Judge Turner and Judge Twisden coming that circuit, I was brought before Judge Twisden, the 14th of the month called March, the latter end of the year 1663.

When I was brought to the bar, I said, "Peace be amongst you all." The Judge looked upon me, and said, "What! Do you come into the court with your hat on?" Upon which words, the jailer taking it off, I said, "The hat is not the honor that comes from God."

Then said the Judge to me, "Will you take the oath of allegiance, George Fox?" I said, "I never took any oath in my life, nor any covenant or engagement." "Well," said he, "will you swear or no?" I answered, "I am a Christian, and Christ commands me not to swear; so does the apostle James; and whether I should obey God or man, do thou judge."

"I ask you again," said he, "whether you will swear or no." I answered again, "I am neither Turk, Jew, nor heathen, but a Christian, and should show forth Christianity."

I asked him if he did not know that Christians in the primitive times, under the ten persecutions, and some also of the martyrs in Queen Mary's days, refused swearing, because Christ and the apostle had forbidden it. I told him also that they had had experience enough, how many had first sworn for the King and then against him. "But as for me," I said, "I have never taken an oath in my life. My allegiance doth not lie in swearing, but in truth and faithfulness, for I honor all men, much more the King. But Christ, who is the Great Prophet, the King of kings, the Savior and Judge of the whole world, saith I must not swear. Now, must I obey Christ or thee? For it is because of tenderness of conscience, and in obedience to the command of Christ, that I do not swear and we have the word of a King for tender consciences."

Then I asked the Judge if he did own the King. "Yes," said he, "I do own the King."

"Why, then," said I, "dost thou not observe his declaration from Breda, and his promises made since he came into England, that no man should be called in question for matters of religion so long as he lived peaceably? If thou ownest the King," said I, "why dost thou call me in question, and put me upon taking an oath, which is a matter of religion; seeing that neither thou nor any one else can charge me with unpeaceable living?" . . .

Then he roused himself up, and said, "I will not be afraid of thee, George Fox; thou speakest so loud thy voice drowns mine and the court's; I must call for three or four criers to drown thy voice; thou hast good lungs."*

"I am a prisoner here," said I, "for the Lord Jesus Christ's sake; for His sake do I suffer; for Him do I stand this day. If my voice were five times louder, I should lift it up and sound it for Christ's sake. I stand this day before your judgment seat in obedience to Christ, who commands not to swear; before whose judgment seat you must all be brought and must give an account."

"Well," said the Judge, "George Fox, say whether thou wilt take the oath, yea or nay?"

I replied, "I say, as I said before, judge thou whether I ought to obey God or man. If I could take any oath at all I should take this. I do not deny some oaths only, or on some occasions, but all oaths, according to Christ's doctrine, who hath commanded His followers not to swear at all. Now if thou, or any of you, or your ministers or priests here, will prove that ever Christ or His apostles, after they had forbidden all swearing, commanded Christians to swear, then I will swear."

I saw several priests there, but not one of them offered to speak.

---

* The authoritative tones with which Fox spoke were often remarked on. That the judge says he will not be afraid of Fox is remarkable. Each of Fox's persecutors must have worried a bit that they were playing the role of Pilate in the Gospels.

"Then," said the Judge, "I am a servant to the King, and the King sent me not to dispute with you, but to put the laws in execution; therefore tender him the oath of allegiance."

"If thou love the King," said I, "why dost thou break his word, and not keep his declarations and speeches, wherein he promised liberty to tender consciences? I am a man of a tender conscience, and, in obedience to Christ's command, I cannot swear."

"Then you will not swear," said the Judge; "take him away, jailer."

I said, "It is for Christ's sake that I cannot swear, and for obedience to His command I suffer; and so the Lord forgive you all."

So the jailer took me away; but I felt that the mighty power of the Lord was over them all.

The sixteenth day of the same month I was again brought before Judge Twisden. He was somewhat offended at my hat; but it being the last morning of the assize before he was to leave town, and not many people there, he made the less of it. . . .

Then said he, "Take him away; I will have nothing to do with him; take him away." I said, "Well, live in the fear of God, and do justice." "Why," said he, "have I not done you justice?" I replied, "That which thou hast done has been against the command of Christ." So I was taken to the jail again, and kept prisoner till the next assizes.

Some time before this assize Margaret Fell was sent prisoner to Lancaster jail by justices Fleming, Kirby, and Preston, . . . and at the assize the oath was tendered to her also, and she was again committed to prison.

In August . . . the assizes were again held at Lancaster, and the same judges, Twisden and Turner, again came that circuit. But Judge Turner then sat on the crown bench, and so I was brought before him. Before I was called to the bar I was put among the murderers and felons for about two hours, the people, the justices, and also the Judge gazing upon me.

After they had tried several others, they called me to the bar, and empanelled a jury. Then the Judge asked the justices whether they had tendered me the oath at the sessions. They said that they had. Then he said, "Give them the book, that they may swear they tendered him the oath at the sessions." They said they had. Then he said, "Give them the book, that they may swear they tendered him the oath according to the indictment."

Some of the justices refused to be sworn; but the Judge said he would have it done, to take away all occasion of exception. When the jury were sworn, and the justices had sworn that they had tendered me the oath according to the indictment, the Judge asked me whether I had not refused the oath at the last assizes. I said, "I never took an oath in my life, and

Christ the Savior and Judge of the world, said, 'Swear not at all.' " . . .

Then the clerk read the indictment, and I told the Judge I had something to speak to it; for I had informed myself of the errors that were in it. He told me he would hear afterwards any reasons that I could allege why he should not give judgment. Then I spoke to the jury, and told them that they could not bring me in guilty according to that indictment, for the indictment was wrong laid, and had many gross errors in it. . . .

I asked him whether the oath was to be tendered to the King's subjects, or to the subjects of foreign princes. He said, "To the subjects of this realm." "Then," said I, "look into the indictment; ye may see that ye have left out the word 'subject'; so not having named me in the indictment as a subject, ye cannot praemunire* me for not taking an oath." Then they looked over the statute and the indictment, and saw it was as I said; and the Judge confessed it was an error.

I told him I had something else to stop his judgment, and desired him to look what day the indictment said the oath was tendered to me at the sessions there. They looked, and said it was the eleventh day of January. "What day of the week was the sessions held on?" said I. "On a Tuesday," said they. "Then,"

---

* Strip him of all possessions and imprison him under the king's orders.

said I, "look in your almanacs, and see whether there was any sessions held at Lancaster on the eleventh day of January, so called."

So they looked, and found that the eleventh day was the day called Monday, and that the sessions was on the day called Tuesday, which was the twelfth day of that month.

"Look now," said I, "ye have indicted me for refusing the oath in the quarter sessions held at Lancaster on the eleventh day of January last, and the justices have sworn that they tendered me the oath in open sessions here that day, and the jury upon their oaths have found me guilty thereupon; and yet ye see there was no session held in Lancaster that day."

Then the Judge, to cover the matter, asked whether the sessions did not begin on the eleventh day. But some in the court answered, "No; the session held but one day, and that was the twelfth." Then the Judge said this was a great mistake and an error.

Some of the justices were in a great rage at this, stamped, and said, "Who hath done this? Somebody hath done this on purpose"; and a great heat was amongst them.

Then said I, "Are not the justices here, who ... have sworn to this indictment, forsworn men in the face of the country? But this is not all," said I. "I have more yet to offer why sentence should not be given against me." I asked, "In what year of the King was the last assize here holden, which was in the month called March last?" The Judge said it was in the sixteenth year of the King. "But," said I, "the indictment says it was in the fifteenth year." They looked, and found it so. This also was acknowledged to be another error.

Then they were all in a fret again, and could not tell what to say; for the Judge had sworn the officers of the court that the oath was tendered to me at the assize mentioned in the indictment. "Now," said I, "is not the court here forsworn also, who have sworn that the oath was tendered to me at the assize holden here in the fifteenth year of the King, when it was in his sixteenth year, and so they have sworn a year false?"

The Judge bade them look whether Margaret Fell's indictment was so or no. They looked, and found it was not so.

I told the Judge I had more yet to offer to stop sentence; and asked him whether all the oath ought to be put into the indictment or no. "Yes," said he, "it ought to be all put in." "Then," said I, "compare the indictment with the oath, and there thou mayest see these words: viz., 'or by any authority derived, or pretended to be derived from him or his see,' which is a principal part of the oath, left out of the indictment; and in another place the words, 'heirs and successors,' are left out." The Judge acknowledged these also to be great errors.

"But," said I, "I have something further to allege." "Nay," said the Judge, "I have enough; you need say no more." "If," said I, "thou hast enough, I desire nothing but law and justice at thy hands; for I don't look for mercy." "You must have justice," said he, "and you shall have law."

Then I asked, "Am I at liberty, and free from all that ever hath been done against me in this matter?" "Yes," said the Judge, "you are free from all that hath been done against you. But then," starting up in a rage, he said, "I can put the oath to any man here, and I will tender you the oath again." I told him he had had examples enough yesterday of swearing and false swearing, both in the justices and in the jury; for I saw before mine eyes that both justices and jury had forsworn themselves.

The Judge asked me if I would take the oath. I bade him do me justice for my false imprisonment all this while; for what had I been imprisoned so long for? And I told him I ought to be set at liberty. "You are at liberty," said he, "but I will put the oath to you again." Then I turned me about and said, "All people, take notice; this is a snare; for I ought to be set free from the jailer and from this court." But the Judge cried, "Give him the book." And the sheriff and the justices cried, "Give him the book."

Then the power of darkness rose up in them like a mountain, and a clerk lifted up a book to me. I stood still and said, "If it be a Bible, give it me into my hand." "Yes, yes," said the Judge and justices, "give it him into his hand." So I took it and looked into it, and said, "I see it is a Bible; I am glad of it."

. . . He had caused the jury to be called, and they stood by; for, after they had brought in their former verdict, he would not dismiss them, though they desired it; but told them he could not dismiss them yet, for he should have business for them, and therefore they must attend and be ready when they were called.

When he said so I felt his intent, that if I were freed, he would come on again. So I looked him in the face, and the witness of God started up in him, and made him blush when he looked at me again, for he saw that I saw him. Nevertheless, hardening himself, he caused the oath to be read to me, the jury standing by; and when it was read, he asked me whether I would take the oath or not.

Then said I, "Ye have given me a book here to kiss and to swear on, and this book which ye have given me to kiss says, 'Kiss the Son'; and the Son says in this book, 'Swear not at all'; and so says also the apostle James. Now, I say as the book says, and yet ye imprison me; why do ye not imprison the book for saying so? How comes it that the book (which bids me not swear) is at liberty amongst you, and yet ye imprison me for doing as the book bids me?"

As I was speaking this to them, and held up the Bible open in my hand, to show them the place in the book where Christ forbids swearing, they plucked the book out of my hand again; and the Judge said, "Nay, but we will imprison George Fox." Yet this got abroad over all the country as a by-word, that "They gave me a book to swear on that commanded me 'not to swear at all'; and that the Bible was at liberty, and I in prison for doing as the Bible said."

Now, when the Judge still urged me to swear, I told him I had never taken oath, covenant, or engagement in my life, but my yea or nay was more binding to me than an oath was to many others; for had they not had experience how little men regarded an oath; and how they had sworn one way and then another; and how the justices and court had forsworn themselves now? I told him I was a man of a tender conscience, and if they had any sense of a tender conscience they would consider that it was in obedience to Christ's command that I could not swear. "But," said I, "if any of you can convince me that after Christ and the apostle had commanded not to swear, they altered that command and commanded Christians to swear, then ye shall see I will swear."

There being many priests by, I said, "If ye cannot do it, let your priests stand up and do it." But not one of the priests made any answer.

"Oh," said the Judge, "all the world cannot convince you." "No," said I, "how is it likely the world should convince me; for 'the whole world lies in wickedness'; but bring out your spiritual men, as ye call them, to convince me."

Then both the sheriff and the Judge said, "The angel swore in the Revelations." I replied, "When God bringeth His first-begotten Son into the world, He saith, 'Let all the angels of God worship Him'; and He saith, 'Swear not at all.' "

"Nay," said the Judge, "I will not dispute."

Then I spoke to the jury, telling them it was for Christ's sake that I could not swear, and therefore I warned them not to act contrary to the witness of God in their consciences, for before His judgment seat they must all be brought. And I told them that as for plots and persecution for religion and Popery, I do deny them in my heart; for I am a Christian, and shall show forth Christianity amongst you this day. It is for Christ's doctrine I stand. More words I had both with the Judge and jury before the jailer took me away.

In the afternoon I was brought up again, and put among the thieves some time, where I stood with my hat on till the jailer took it off. Then the jury having found this new indictment against me for not taking the oath, I was called to the bar; and the Judge asked me what I would say for myself. I bade them read the indictment, for I would not answer to that which I did not hear. The clerk read it, and as he read the Judge said "Take heed it be not false again"; but he read it in such a manner that I could hardly understand what he read.

When he had done the Judge asked me what I said to the indictment. I told him that hearing but once so large a writing . . . and at such a distance that I could not distinctly hear all the parts of it, I could not well tell what to say to it; but if he would let me have a copy, and give me time to consider it, I would answer it. . . . After awhile the Judge asked me, "What time would you have?" I said, "Until the next assize." . . .

After some further discourse they committed me to prison again, there to lie until the next assize; and Colonel Kirby gave order to the jailer to keep me close, "and suffer no flesh alive to come at me," for I was not fit, he said, "to be discoursed with by men." I was put into a tower where the smoke of the other prisoners came up so thick it stood as dew upon the walls, and sometimes it was so thick that I could hardly see the candle when it burned; and I being locked under three locks, the under-jailer, when the smoke was great, would hardly be persuaded to come up to unlock one of the uppermost doors for fear of the smoke, so that I was almost smothered.

Besides, it rained in upon my bed, and many times, when I went to stop out the rain in the cold winter season, my shirt was as wet as muck with the rain that came in upon me while I was laboring to stop it out.

And the place being high and open to the wind, sometimes as fast as I stopped it the wind blew it out again. In this manner I lay all that long, cold winter till the next assize, in which time I was so starved, and so frozen with cold and wet with the rain that my body was greatly swelled and my limbs much benumbed.

The assize began the sixteenth of the month called March, 1664–1665. The same Judges, Twisden and Turner, coming that circuit again, Judge Twisden sat this time on the crown bench, and before him I was brought.

I had informed myself of the errors in this indictment also; for, though at the assize before Judge Turner said to the officers in court, "Pray, see that all the oath be in the indictment, and that the word 'subject' be in, and that the day of the month and year of the King be put in right; for it is a shame that so many errors should be seen and found in the face of the country"; yet many errors, and those great ones, were in this indictment, as well as in the former. Surely the hand of the Lord was in it, to confound their mischievous work against me, and to blind them therein; insomuch that, although, after the indictment was drawn at the former assize, the Judge examined it himself, and tried it with the clerks, yet the word "subject" was left out of this indictment also, the day of the month was put in wrong, and several material words of the oath were left out; yet they went on confidently against me, thinking all was safe and well.

When I was brought to the bar, and the jury called over to be sworn, the clerk asked me, first, whether I had any objection to make to any of the jury. I told him I knew none of them. Then, having sworn the jury, they swore three of the officers of the court to prove that the oath was tendered to me at the last assizes, according to the indictment.

"Come, come," said the Judge, "it was not done in a corner." Then he asked me what I had to say to it; or whether I had taken the oath at the last assize. I told him what I had formerly said to them, as it now came to my remembrance. Thereupon the Judge said, "I will not dispute with you but in point of law." "Then," said I, "I have something to speak to the jury concerning the indictment." He told me I must not speak to the jury; but if I had anything to say, I must speak to him.

I asked him whether the oath was to be tendered to the King's subjects only, or to the subjects of foreign princes. He replied, "To the subjects of this realm." "Then," said I, "look in the indictment, and thou may-est see the word 'subject' is left out of this indictment also. Therefore, seeing the oath is not to be tendered to any but the subjects of this realm, and ye have not put me in as a subject, the court is to take no notice of this indictment."

I had no sooner spoken thus than the Judge cried, "Take him away, jailer, take him away." So I was pres-ently hurried away. The jailer and people expected that I should be called for again; but I was never brought to the court any more, though I had many other great errors to assign in the indictment.

After I was gone, the Judge asked the jury if they were agreed. They said, "Yes," and found for the King against me, as I was told. But I was never called to hear sentence given, nor was any given against me that I could hear of.

I understood that when they had looked more narrowly into the indictment they saw it was not good; and the Judge having sworn the officers of the court that the oath was tendered me at the assize before, such a day, as was set forth in the indictment, and that being the wrong day, I should have proved the officers of the court forsworn men again, had the Judge suffered me to plead to the indictment, which was thought to be the reason he hurried me away so soon.

The Judge had passed sentence of praemunire* upon Margaret Fell before I was brought in; and it seems that when I was hurried away they recorded me as a praemunired person, though I was never brought to hear the sentence, or knew of it, which was very illegal. . . .

. . . As I was walking in my chamber, with my eye to the Lord, I saw the angel of the Lord with a glittering drawn sword stretched southward, as though

---

* Loss of possessions and imprisonment by the king. Mrs. Fell had wealth, so this was a double sentence. But as we shall see, she did not actually lose her possessions.

the court had been all on fire. Not long after the wars broke out with Holland, the sickness broke forth, and afterwards the fire of London; so the Lord's sword was drawn indeed.

By reason of my long and close imprisonment in so bad a place I . . . had become very weak in body; but the Lord's power was over all, supported me through all, and enabled me to do service for Him, and for His truth and people, as the place would admit. For, while I was in Lancaster prison, I rebutted . . . several books, . . . namely the Catholic Mass, the Anglican Common Prayer, the Presbyterian Directory and the Congregational Church Faith, which are used by the four chief religions that are got up since the apostles' days.

Chapter Sixteen

A Year in Scarborough Castle

(1665–1666)

ABOUT SIX WEEKS after the assizes they
got an order from the King and council
to remove me from Lancaster; and with
it they brought a letter from the Earl of Anglesey,
wherein it was written that if those things with which
I was charged were found true against me, I deserved
no clemency nor mercy. . . .

When they had prepared for my removal, the
under-sheriff and the head-sheriff's man, with some
bailiffs, fetched me out of the castle, when I was so
weak with lying in that cold, wet, and smoky prison,

that I could hardly go or stand. They led me into the jailer's house, where were William Kirby and several others, and they called for wine to give me. I told them I would have none of their wine. Then they cried, "Bring out the horses."

I desired them first to show me their order, or a copy of it, if they intended to remove me; but they would show me none but their swords. I told them there was no sentence passed upon me, nor was I praemunired, that I knew of; and therefore I was not made the King's prisoner, but was the sheriff's; for they and all the country knew that I was not fully heard at the last assize, nor suffered to show the errors in the indictment, which were sufficient to quash it, though they had kept me from one assize to another to the end they might try me. But they all knew there was no sentence of praemunire passed upon me; therefore I, not being the King's prisoner, but the sheriff's, did desire to see their order. Instead of showing me their order, they haled me out, and lifted me upon one of the sheriff's horses. . . .

They hurried me away about fourteen miles to Bentham, though I was so weak that I was hardly able to sit on horseback, and my clothes smelt so of smoke they were loathsome to myself. The wicked jailer, one Hunter, a young fellow, would come behind and give the horse a lash with his whip, and make him skip and leap; so that I, being weak, had much ado to sit on him; then he would come and look me in the face and say, "How do you, Mr. Fox?" I told him it was not civil in him to do so. The Lord cut him off soon after. . . .

They kept me at York two days, and then the marshal and four or five soldiers were sent to convey me to Scarborough Castle. . . . Next . . . they conducted me into the castle, put me into a room, and set a sentry on me. As I was very weak, and subject to fainting, they sometimes let me go out into the air with the sentry. They soon removed me out of this room, and put me into an open one, where the rain came in, and which was exceedingly thick with smoke, which was very offensive to me.

One day the Governor, Sir John Crossland, came to see me, and brought with him Sir Francis Cobb. I desired the Governor to go into my room, and see what a place I had. I had got a little fire made in it, and it was so filled with smoke that when they were in they could hardly find their way out again; and he being a Papist, I told him that this was his Purgatory which they had put me into. I was forced to lay out about fifty shillings to stop out the rain, and keep the room from smoking so much.

When I had been at that charge, and made it tolerable, they removed me into a worse room, where I had neither chimney nor fire hearth. This being towards the seaside and lying much open, the wind drove in the rain forcibly so that the water came over my bed, and ran so about the room that I was fain to skim it up with a platter. When my clothes were wet, I had no fire to dry them; so that my body was benumbed with cold, and my fingers swelled so that one was grown as big as two.

Though I was at some charge in this room also, I could not keep out the wind and rain. Besides, they would suffer few Friends to come to me, and many times not any; no, not so much as to bring me a little food; but I was forced for the first quarter to hire one of another society to bring me necessaries. Sometimes the soldiers would take it from her, and she would scuffle with them for it.

Afterwards I hired a soldier to fetch me water and bread, and something to make a fire of, when I was in a room where a fire could be made. Commonly a threepenny loaf served me three weeks, and sometimes longer, and most of my drink was water with wormwood steeped or bruised in it. . . .

But though they would not let Friends come to me, they would often bring others, either to gaze upon me, or to contend with me. One time a great company of Papists came to discourse with me. They affirmed that the Pope was infallible, and had stood infallible ever since Peter's time. But I showed them the contrary by history; for one of the bishops of Rome (Marcellinus by name), denied the faith and sacrificed to idols; therefore he was not infallible. I told them that if they were in the infallible Spirit, they need not have jails, swords, and staves, racks and tortures, fires and fag-gots, whips and gallows, to hold up their religion, and to destroy men's lives about it; for if they were in the infallible Spirit, they would preserve men's lives, and use none but spiritual weapons about religion.

Another Papist who came to discourse with me said, "All the patriarchs were in hell from the creation till Christ came. When Christ suffered He went into hell, and the devil said to Him, 'What comest thou hither for? To break open our strongholds?' And Christ said, 'To fetch them all out.' So Christ was three days and three nights in hell to bring them out."

I told him that that was false; for Christ said to the thief, "This day thou shalt be with me in paradise"; and Enoch and Elijah were translated into heaven; and Abraham was in heaven, for the Scripture saith that Lazarus was in his bosom; and Moses and Elias were with Christ upon the Mount, before He suf-fered. These instances stopped the Papist's mouth, and put him to a stand.

Another time came Dr. Witty, who was esteemed a great doctor in physic, with Lord Falconbridge, the governor of Tinmouth Castle, and several knights. I being called to them, Witty undertook to discourse with me, and asked me what I was in prison for. I told him, "Because I would not disobey the command of Christ, and swear." He said I ought to swear my alle-giance to the King.

He being a great Presbyterian, I asked him whether he had not sworn against the King and House of Lords, and taken the Scotch covenant? And had he not since sworn to the King? What, then, was his swearing good for? But my allegiance, I told him, did not consist in swearing, but in truth and faithfulness.

After some further discourse I was taken away to my prison again; and afterwards Dr. Witty boasted in the town amongst his patients that he had conquered me. When I heard of it, I told the Governor it was a small boast in him to say he had conquered a bond-man. I desired to bid him come to me again when he came to the Castle.

He came again awhile after, with about sixteen or seventeen great persons, and then he ran himself worse on ground than before. For he affirmed before them all that Christ had not enlightened every man that cometh into the world; and that the grace of God, that bringeth salvation, had not appeared unto all men, and that Christ had not died for all men.

I asked him what sort of men those were whom Christ had not enlightened? And whom His grace had not appeared to? And whom He had not died for? He said, "Christ did not die for adulterers, and idolaters, and wicked men." I asked him whether adulterers and wicked men were not sinners. He said, "Yes." "Did not Christ die for sinners?" said I. "Did He not come to call sinners to repentance?"

"Yes," said he. "Then," said I, "thou hast stopped thy own mouth." So I proved that the grace of God had appeared unto all men, though some turned from it into wantonness, and walked despitefully against it; and that Christ had enlightened all men, though some hated the light. Several of the people confessed it was true; but Witty . . . went away in a great rage, and came no more to me. . . .

There came another time the widow of old Lord Fairfax, and with her a great company, one of whom was a priest. I was moved to declare the truth to them, and the priest asked me why we said Thou and Thee to people, for he counted us but fools and idiots for speaking so.

I asked him whether they that translated the Scriptures and that made the grammar . . . , were fools and idiots, seeing they translated the Scriptures so, and made the grammar so, Thou to one, and You to more than one, and left it so to us. If they were fools and idiots, why had not he, and such as he, that looked upon themselves as wise men, and that could not bear Thou and Thee to a singular, altered the grammar . . . and Bible, and put the plural instead of the singular. But if they were wise men who . . . had so translated the Bible, and had made the grammar . . . so, I wished him to consider whether they were not fools and idiots themselves, who . . . did not speak as their grammars and Bibles taught them; but were offended with us, and called us fools and idiots for speaking so.

Thus the priest's mouth was stopped, and many of the company acknowledged the Truth, and were pretty loving and tender. Some of them would have given me money, but I would not receive it.

After this came Dr. Cradock, with three priests more, and the Governor and his lady (so called), and another that was called a lady, and a great company with them. . . . I asked him why he persecuted Friends for not paying tithes; whether God ever commanded the Gentiles to pay tithes; whether Christ had not ended tithes when He ended the Levitical priesthood that took tithes; whether Christ, when He sent His disciples to preach, had not commanded them to preach freely as He had given them freely; and whether all the ministers of Christ are not bound to observe this command of Christ. He said he would not dispute that.

Neither did I find he was willing to stay on that subject; for he presently turned to another matter, and said, "You marry, but I know not how." I replied, "It may be so; but why dost thou not come and see?"

Then he threatened that he would use his power against us, as he had done. I bade him take heed; for he was an old man. I asked him also where he read, from Genesis to Revelation, that ever any priest did marry any. I wished him to show me some instance thereof if he would have us come to them to be married; "for," said I, "thou hast excommunicated one of my friends two years after he was dead, about his marriage. And why dost thou not excommunicate Isaac, and Jacob, and Boaz, and Ruth? For we do not read that they were ever married by the priests; but they took one another in the assemblies of the righteous, in the presence of God and His people; and so do we. So that we have all the holy men and women that the Scripture speaks of in this practice, on our side." . . .

The officers often threatened that I should be hanged over the wall. Nay, the deputy governor told me once that the King, knowing I had many followers . . . in the people, had sent me thither, that if there should be any stirring in the nation, they should hang me over the wall to keep the people down.

There being, awhile after, a marriage at a Baptist's house, upon which occasion a great many of them were met together, they talked much then of hanging me. But I told them that if that was what they desired, and it was permitted them, I was ready, for I never feared death nor sufferings in my life; but I was known to be an innocent, peaceable man, free from all stirrings and plottings, and one that sought the good of all men. . . .

There were great imprisonments in this and the former years, while I was prisoner at Lancaster and Scarborough. At London many Friends were crowded into Newgate, and other prisons, where the sickness was,* and many died in prison. Many also were banished, and several sent on shipboard[†] by the King's order. . . . But in time the Lord's power wrought over this storm, and many of our persecutors were confounded and put to shame.

After I had lain prisoner above a year in Scarborough Castle, I sent a letter to the King, in which I gave him an account of my imprisonment, and the bad usage I had received in prison; and also that I was informed no man could deliver me but him. After this, John Whitehead being at London, and having acquaintance also with Esquire Marsh, he went to visit him, and spoke to him about me; and he undertook, if John Whitehead would get the state of my case drawn up, to deliver it to the master of requests, Sir John Birkenhead, who would endeavor to get a release for me.

So John Whitehead and Ellis Hookes drew up a relation of my imprisonment and sufferings, and carried it to Marsh; and he went with it to the master of requests, who procured an order from the King for my release. The substance of the order was that "the King, being certainly informed that I was a man principled against plotting and fighting, and had been

---

* The London plague of 1665.

† Forced to work as virtual slaves on ships.

ready at all times to discover plots, rather than to make any, etc., therefore his royal pleasure was that I should be discharged from my imprisonment," etc.

As soon as this order was obtained, John Whitehead came to Scarborough with it, and delivered it to the Governor; who, upon receipt thereof, gathered the officers together, and, without requiring bond or sureties for my peaceable living, being satisfied that I was a man of a peaceable life, he discharged me freely. . . .

The very next day after my release, the fire broke out in London, and the report of it came quickly down into the country. Then I saw the Lord God was true and just in His Word, which he had shown me before in Lancaster jail, when I saw the angel of the Lord with a glittering sword drawn southward. . . .

Indeed, I could not but take notice how the hand of the Lord turned against the persecutors who had been the cause of my imprisonment, or had been abusive or cruel to me in it. The officer that fetched me to Holker Hall wasted his estate, and soon after fled into Ireland. Most of the justices that were upon the bench at the sessions when I was sent to prison, died in awhile after; as old Thomas Preston, Rawlinson, Porter, and Matthew West, of Borwick. Justice Fleming's wife died, and left him thirteen or fourteen motherless children. Colonel Kirby never prospered after. The chief constable, Richard Dodgson, died soon after, and Mount, the petty constable, and the wife of the other petty constable, John Ashburn-ham, who railed at me in her house, died soon after. William Knipe, the witness they brought against me, died soon after also. Hunter, the jailer of Lancaster, who was very wicked to me while I was his prisoner, was cut off in his young days; and the under-sheriff that carried me from Lancaster prison towards Scar-borough, lived not long after. And Joblin, the jailer of Durham, who was prisoner with me in Scarborough Castle, and had often incensed the Governor and sol-diers against me, though he got out of prison, yet the Lord cut him off in his wickedness soon after.

When I came into that country again, most of those that dwelt in Lancashire were dead, and others ruined in their estates; so that, though I did not seek revenge upon them for their acting against me con-trary to the law, yet the Lord had executed His judg-ments upon many of them.

Chapter Seventeen

At the Work of Organizing
(1667–1670)

THEN I WAS moved of the Lord to recommend the setting up of five monthly meetings of men and women in the city of London (besides the previous women's meetings and the quarterly meetings), to take care of God's glory, and to admonish and exhort such as walked disorderly or carelessly, and not according to Truth. For whereas Friends had had only quarterly meetings, now that Truth was spread, and Friends were grown more numerous, I was moved to recommend the setting up of monthly meetings throughout the nation.

And the Lord opened to me what I must do, and how the men's and women's monthly and quarterly meetings should be ordered and established in this and in other nations; and that I should write to those where I did not come, to do the same.

After things were well settled at London, and the Lord's Truth, power, seed, and life reigned and shone over all in the city, I went into Essex. . . . I was so exceeding weak, I was hardly able to get on or off my horse's back; but my spirit being earnestly engaged in the work the Lord had concerned me in and sent me forth about, I traveled on therein, notwithstanding the weakness of my body, having confidence in the Lord, that He would carry me through, as He did by His power. . . .

I wrote also into Ireland by faithful Friends, and into Scotland, Holland, Barbados, and several parts of America, advising Friends to settle their men's monthly meetings in those countries. For they had had their general quarterly meetings before; but now that Truth was increased amongst them, it was needful that they should settle those men's monthly meetings in the power and Spirit of God. . . .

Now [1669] was I moved of the Lord to go over into Ireland, to visit the Seed of God in that nation. There went with me Robert Lodge, James Lancaster, Thomas Briggs, and John Stubbs. . . . When we came before Dublin, we took boat and went ashore; and the earth and air smelt, methought, of the corruption of the nation, so that it yielded another smell to me than England did; which I imputed to the Popish massacres that had been committed, and the blood that had been spilt in it, from which a foulness ascended. . . .

He that was then mayor of Cork, being very envious against Truth and Friends, had many Friends in prison. Knowing I was in the country, he sent four warrants to take me; therefore Friends were desirous that I should not ride through Cork. But, being at Bandon, there appeared to me in a vision a very ugly-visaged man, of a black and dark look. My spirit struck at him in the power of God, and it seemed to me that I rode over him with my horse, and my horse set his foot on the side of his face.

When I came down in the morning, I told a friend the command of the Lord to me was to ride through Cork; but I bade him tell no man. So we took horse, many Friends being with me. When we came near the town, Friends would have shown me a way through the back side of it; but I told them my way was through the streets. Taking Paul Morrice to guide me through the town, I rode on.

As we rode through the marketplace, and by the mayor's door, he, seeing me, said, "There goes George Fox"; but he had not power to stop me. When we had passed the sentinels, and were come over the bridge, we went to a Friend's house and alighted. There the

Friends told me what a rage was in the town, and how many warrants were granted to take me. . . .

Great was the rage that the mayor and others of Cork were in that they had missed me, and great pains they afterwards took to catch me, having their scouts abroad upon the roads, as I understood, to observe which way I went. . . .

One very envious magistrate, who was both a priest and a justice, got a warrant from the Judge of assize to apprehend me. The warrant was to go over all his circuit, which reached near a hundred miles. Yet the Lord disappointed all their councils, defeated all their designs against me, and by His good hand of Providence preserved me out of all their snares, and gave us many sweet and blessed opportunities to visit Friends, and spread Truth through that nation.

Our . . . meetings were very large, Friends coming to them from far and near; and other people flocking in. The powerful presence of the Lord was preciously felt amongst us. Many of the world were reached, convinced, and gathered to the Truth; the Lord's flock was increased; and Friends were greatly refreshed and comforted in feeling the love of God. . . .

After I had traveled over Ireland, and visited Friends in their meetings, as well for business as for worship, and had answered several papers and writings from monks, friars, and Protestant priests, . . . I returned to Dublin, in order to take passage for England. . . .

We traveled till we came to Bristol, where I met with Margaret Fell, who was come to visit her daughter Yeomans.

I had seen from the Lord a considerable time before, that I should take Margaret Fell to be my wife. And when I first mentioned it to her, she felt the answer of Life from God thereunto. But though the Lord had opened this thing to me, yet I had not received a command from the Lord for the accomplishing of it then. Wherefore I let the thing rest, and went on in the work and service of the Lord as before, according as he led me; traveling up and down in this nation, and through Ireland.

But now being at Bristol, and finding Margaret Fell there, it opened in me from the Lord that the thing should be accomplished. After we had discoursed the matter together, I told her, if she also was satisfied with the accomplishing of it now, she should first send for her children; which she did. When the rest of her daughters were come, I asked both them and her sons-in-law if they had anything against it, or for it; and they all severally expressed their satisfaction therein.

Then I asked Margaret if she had fulfilled and performed her husband's will to her children. She replied, "The children know that." Whereupon I asked them whether, if their mother married, they would lose by it. . . .

The children said she had answered it to them, and desired me to speak no more of it. I told them I was plain, and would have all things done plainly; for I sought not any outward advantage to myself.

So, after I had thus acquainted the children with it, our intention of marriage was laid before Friends, both privately and publicly, to their full satisfaction. Many of them gave testimony thereunto that it was of God.... Then was a certificate,* relating both the proceedings and the marriage, openly read, and signed by the relations, and by most of the ancient Friends of that city, besides many others from diverse parts of the nation.

We stayed about a week in Bristol, and then went together to Oldstone: where, taking leave of each other in the Lord, we parted, betaking ourselves each to our several service; Margaret returning homewards to the north, and I passing on in the work of the Lord as before.† I traveled through Wiltshire, Berkshire, Oxfordshire, Buckinghamshire, and so to London, visiting Friends; in all of which counties I had many large and precious meetings.

[In 1670 the so-called Conventicle Act, originally passed in 1664, was renewed with increased vigor. The Act limited religious gatherings, other than those of

---

* Dated "Eighth month" 27th, 1669.

† They were mostly separated for four years. During some of that time, Margaret, now Margaret Fox, was imprisoned in Lancashire. Shortly after her release, Fox was scheduled to travel to America.

the Established Church, to five persons, and brought all who refused to take an oath under the penalties of the Act.]

On the First-day after the Act came in force, I went to the meeting at Gracechurch Street, where I expected the storm was most likely to begin. . . . After I had spoken awhile to this effect, the constable came with an informer and soldiers; and as they pulled me down, I said, "Blessed are the peacemakers." . . .

When we were come to the mayor's house, and were in the courtyard, several of the people that stood about, asked me how and for what I was taken. . . . When the mayor came, we were brought into the room where he was, and some of his officers would have taken off our hats, perceiving which he called to them, and bade them let us alone, and not meddle with our hats; "for," said he, "they are not yet brought before me in judicature." So we stood by while he examined some Presbyterian and Baptist teachers; with whom he was somewhat sharp, and convicted them.

After he had done with them, I was brought up to the table where he sat; and then the officers took off my hat. The mayor said mildly to me, "Mr. Fox, you are an eminent man amongst those of your profession; pray, will you be instrumental to dissuade them from meeting in such great numbers? For, seeing Christ hath promised that where two or three are met in His name, He will be in the midst of them, and the

King and Parliament are graciously pleased to allow four to meet together to worship God; why will not you be content to partake both of Christ's promise to two or three, and the King's indulgence to four?"

I answered to this purpose: "Christ's promise was not to discourage many from meeting together in His name, but to encourage the few, that the fewest might not forbear to meet because of their fewness. But if Christ hath promised to manifest His presence in the midst of so small an assembly, where but two or three are gathered in His name, how much more would His presence abound where two or three hundred are gathered in His name?"

I wished him to consider whether this Act, if it had been in their time, would not have taken hold of Christ, with His twelve apostles and seventy disciples, who used to meet often together, and that with great numbers? However, I told him this Act did not concern us; for it was made against seditious meetings, of such as met under color and pretense of religion "to contrive insurrections, as [the Act says] late experience had shown." But we had been sufficiently tried and proved, and always found peaceable, and therefore he would do well to put a difference between the innocent and the guilty.

He said the Act was made against meetings, and a worship not according to the liturgy. I told him "according to" was not the very same thing; and asked him whether the liturgy was according to the Scriptures, and whether we might not read Scriptures and speak Scriptures. He said, "Yes." I told him, "This Act takes hold only of such as meet to plot and contrive insurrections, as late experience hath shown; but they have never experienced that by us." . . .

After some more discourse, he took our names and the places where we lodged; and at length, as the informer was gone, he set us at liberty. . . . But this . . . mayor, whose name was Samuel Starling, though he carried himself smoothly towards us, proved afterwards a very great persecutor of our Friends, many of whom he cast into prison, as may be seen in the trials of William Penn,* William Mead, and others, at the Old Bailey this year of 1670.

As I was walking down a hill, near Rochester, a great weight and oppression fell upon my spirit. I got on my horse again, but the weight remained so that I was hardly able to ride. At length we came to Rochester, but I was much spent, being so extremely laden and burthened with the world's spirits, that my life was oppressed under them. I got with difficulty to Gravesend, and lay at an inn there; but could hardly either eat or sleep. . . .

. . . After this . . . I rode with great uneasiness to Stratford, to a Friend's house, whose name was Williams,

---

* Founder of Pennsylvania and both a rich and prominent person.

and who had formerly been a captain. Here I lay, exceedingly weak, and at last lost both hearing and sight. . . . Under great sufferings and travails, sorrows and oppressions, I lay for several weeks, whereby I was brought so low and weak in body that few thought I could live. . . .

Though it was a cruel, bloody, persecuting time, yet the Lord's power went over all, His everlasting Seed prevailed; and Friends were made to stand firm and faithful in the Lord's power. Some sober people of other professions would say, "If Friends did not stand, the nation would run into debauchery." . . .

After some time it pleased the Lord to allay the heat of this violent persecution; and I felt . . . an over-coming of the spirits of those men-eaters who . . . had stirred it up and carried it on to that height of cru-elty. I was outwardly very weak; and I plainly felt, and those Friends that were with me, and that came to visit me, took notice, that as the persecution ceased I came from under the travails and sufferings that had lain with such weight upon me; so that towards the spring I began to recover, and to walk up and down, beyond the expectation of many, who did not think I could ever have gone abroad again. . . .

Chapter Eighteen

Two Years in America
(1671–1673)

W HEN I RECEIVED notice of my wife's being taken to prison again,* I sent two of her daughters to the King, and they procured his order to the sheriff of Lancashire for her discharge. But though I expected she would have been set at liberty, yet this violent storm of persecution coming suddenly on, the persecutors there found means to hold her still in prison.

---

* In 1669, about three months after the marriage. The sentence of *praemunire* was passed against Margaret Fell in 1663, but apparently her possessions, while at risk, had not been confiscated, as we see in the next paragraph.

But now the persecution a little ceasing, I was moved to speak to Martha Fisher, and another woman Friend, to go to the King about her liberty. They went in the faith, and in the Lord's power; and He gave them favor with the King, so that he granted a discharge under the broad seal, to clear both her and her estate, after she had been ten years a prisoner, and praemunired; the like whereof was scarce to be heard in England.

I sent down the discharge forthwith by a Friend; by whom also I wrote to her, to inform her how to get it delivered to the justices, and also to acquaint her that it was upon me from the Lord to go beyond sea, to visit the plantations in America; and therefore I desired her to hasten to London, as soon as she could conveniently after she had obtained her liberty, because the ship was then fitting for the voyage. . . .

We then went from Wapping in a barge to the ship, which lay a little below Gravesend, and there we found the Friends that were bound for the voyage with me, who had gone down to the ship the night before. . . .

In the afternoon, the wind serving, I took leave of my wife and other Friends, and went on board. Before we could sail, there being two of the King's frigates riding in the Downs, the captain of one of them sent his press master on board us, who took three of our seamen. This would certainly have delayed, if not wholly prevented, our voyage, had not the captain of the other frigate, being informed of the leakiness of our vessel, and the length of our voyage, in compassion and much civility, spared us two of his own men.

Before this was over, a customhouse officer came on board to peruse packets and get fees; so that we were kept from sailing till about sunset; during which delay a very considerable number of merchantmen, outward bound, were several leagues before us.

Being clear, we set sail in the evening, and next morning overtook part of that fleet about the height of Dover. We soon reached the rest, and in a little time left them all behind; for our yacht was counted a very swift sailer. But she was very leaky, so that the seamen and some of the passengers did, for the most part, pump day and night. One day they observed that in two hours' time she sucked in sixteen inches of water in the well.

When we had been about three weeks at sea, one afternoon we spied a vessel about four leagues astern of us. Our master said it was a Sallee man-of-war,* that seemed to give us chase. He said, "Come, let us go to supper, and when it grows dark we shall lose him." This he spoke to please and pacify the passengers, some of whom began to be very apprehensive of the danger. But Friends were well satisfied in themselves, having faith in God, and no fear upon their spirits. . . .

---

* A Moorish pirate ship, named for Sallee, in Morocco.

At night the master and others came into my cabin, and asked me what they should do. I told them I was no mariner; and I asked them what they thought was best to do. They said there were but two ways, either to outrun him, or to tack about, and hold the same course we were going before. I told them that if he were a thief, they might be sure he would tack about too; and as for outrunning him, it was to no purpose to talk of that, for they saw he sailed faster than we. They asked me again what they should do, "For," they said, "if the mariners had taken Paul's counsel, they had not come to the damage they did." I answered that it was a trial of faith, and therefore the Lord was to be waited on for counsel.

So, retiring in spirit, the Lord showed me that His life and power were placed between us and the ship that pursued us. I told this to the master and the rest, and that the best way was to tack about and steer our right course. I desired them also to put out all their candles but the one they steered by, and to speak to all the passengers to be still and quiet.

About eleven at night the watch called and said they were just upon us. This disquieted some of the passengers. I sat up in my cabin, and, looking through the porthole, the moon being not quite down, I saw them very near us. I was getting up to go out of the cabin; but remembering the word of the Lord, that His life and power were placed between us and them, I lay down again.

The master and some of the seamen came again, and asked me if they might not steer such a point. I told them they might do as they would.

By this time the moon was quite down. A fresh gale arose, and the Lord hid us from them; we sailed briskly on and saw them no more.

The next day, being the first day of the week, we had a public meeting in the ship, as we usually had on that day throughout the voyage, and the Lord's presence was greatly among us. I desired the people to remember the mercies of the Lord, who had delivered them; for they might have been all in the Turks' hands by that time, had not the Lord's hand saved them. . . .

The third of the Eighth month, early in the morning, we discovered the island of Barbados; but it was between nine and ten at night ere we came to anchor in Carlisle bay. We got on shore as soon as we could, and I with some others walked to the house of a Friend, a merchant, whose name was Richard Forstall, above a quarter of a mile from the bridge. But being very ill and weak, I was so tired, that I was in a manner spent by the time I got thither. There I abode very ill several days, and though they several times gave me things to make me sweat, they could not effect it. What they gave me did rather parch and dry up my body, and made me probably worse than otherwise I might have been.

Thus I continued about three weeks after I landed, having much pain in my bones, joints, and whole body, so that I could hardly get any rest; yet I was pretty cheery, and my spirit kept above it all. Neither did my illness take me off from the service of Truth; but both while I was at sea, and after I came to Barbados, before I was able to travel about, I gave forth several papers (having a Friend to write for me), some of which I sent by the first conveyance for England to be printed.

Soon after I came into the island, I was informed of a remarkable passage, wherein the justice of God did eminently appear. It was thus. There was a young man of Barbados whose name was John Drakes, a person of some note in the world's account, but a common swearer and a bad man, who, when he was in London, had a mind to marry a Friend's daughter, left by her mother very young, with a considerable portion, to the care and government of several Friends, whereof I was one. He made application to me that he might have my consent to marry this young maid.

I told him I was one of her overseers, appointed by her mother, who was a widow, to take care of her; that if her mother had intended her for a match to any man of another profession, she would have disposed her accordingly; but she committed her to us, that she might be trained up in the fear of the Lord; and therefore I should betray the trust reposed in me if I should consent that he, who was out of the fear of God, should marry her; and this I would not do.

When he saw that he could not obtain his desire, he returned to Barbados with great offense of mind against me, but without a just cause. Afterwards, when he heard I was coming to Barbados, he swore desperately, and threatened that if he could possibly procure it, he would have me burned to death when I came there. A Friend hearing of this asked him what I had done to him that he was so violent against me. He would not answer, but said again, "I'll have him burned." Whereupon the Friend replied, "Do not march on too furiously, lest thou come too soon to thy journey's end."

About ten days after he was struck with a violent, burning fever, of which he died; by which his body was so scorched that the people said it was as black as a coal; and three days before I landed his body was laid in the dust. This was taken notice of as a sad example. . . .

. . . But after I had been above a month upon the island my spirit became somewhat easier; I began to recover my health and strength, and to get abroad among Friends. After I was able to go about, and had been a little amongst Friends, . . . I went to visit the Governor, Lewis Morice, Thomas Rous, and some other Friends being with me. He received us very civilly, and treated us very kindly, making us dine with him, and keeping us the greater part of the day before he let us go away. . . .*

We then had a quick and easy passage to Jamaica, where we met again with . . . Friends James Lancaster, John Cartwright, and George Pattison, who had been laboring there in the service of Truth; into which we forthwith entered with them, traveling up and down through the island, which is large; and a brave country it is, though the people are, many of them, debauched and wicked.

We had much service. There was a great convincement, and many received the Truth, some of whom were people of account in the world. We had many meetings there, which were large, and very quiet. The people were civil to us, so that not a mouth was opened against us. I was twice with the Governor, and some other magistrates, who all carried themselves kindly towards me. . . .

When we had been about seven weeks in Jamaica, had brought Friends into pretty good order, and settled several meetings amongst them, we left Solomon Eccles there; the rest of us embarked for Maryland, leaving Friends and Truth prosperous in

---

* While in Barbados, Fox confronted and commented on slavery:

> I desired them also that they would cause their overseers to deal mildly and gently with their negroes, and not use cruelty towards them as the manner of some hath been and is; and that after certain years of servitude, they would make them free.

Jamaica, the Lord's power being over all, and His blessed Seed reigning. . . .

We went on board on the 8th of First month,* 1671–1672, and, having contrary winds, were a full week sailing forwards and backwards before we could get out of sight of Jamaica. A difficult voyage this proved, and dangerous, especially in passing through the Gulf of Florida, where we met with many trials by winds and storms. . . .

For when the winds were so strong and boisterous, and the storms and tempests so great that the sailors knew not what to do, but let the ship go which way she would, then did we pray unto the Lord, who graciously heard us, calmed the winds and the seas, gave us seasonable weather, and made us to rejoice in His salvation. Blessed and praised be the holy name of the Lord, whose power hath dominion over all, whom the winds and the seas obey. . . .

We partook also of another great deliverance in this voyage, through the good providence of the Lord, which we came to understand afterwards. For when we were determined to come from Jamaica, we had our choice of two vessels, that were both bound for the same coast. One of these was a frigate, the other a yacht. The master of the frigate, we thought, asked unreasonably for our passage, which made us agree

---

* March 8, 1672.

with the master of the yacht, who offered to carry us ten shillings apiece cheaper than the other.

We went on board the yacht, and the frigate came out together with us, intending to be consorts during the voyage. For several days we sailed together; but, with calms and contrary winds, we were soon separated. After that the frigate, losing her way, fell among the Spaniards, by whom she was taken and plundered, and the master and mate made prisoners. Afterwards, being retaken by the English, she was sent home to her owners in Virginia. When we came to understand this we saw and admired the providence of God, who preserved us out of our enemies' hands; and he that was covetous fell among the covetous. . . .

After this we went to Maryland . . . , where another general meeting was appointed. We went some of the way by land, the rest by water, and, a storm arising, our boat was run aground, in danger of being beaten to pieces, and the water came in upon us. I was in a great sweat, having come very hot out of a meeting before, and now was wet with the water besides; yet, having faith in the divine power, I was preserved from taking hurt, blessed be the Lord!

To this meeting came many who received the Truth with reverence. We had also a men's meeting and a women's meeting. Most of the backsliders came in again; and several meetings were established for taking care of the affairs of the Church. . . .

There many people received the Truth with gladness, and Friends were greatly refreshed. . . . Several persons of quality in that country attended a meeting . . . two of whom were justices of the peace. It was upon me from the Lord to send to the Indian emperor and his kings to come too. . . . The emperor came. . . .

. . . We then began our journey by land to New England; a tedious journey through the woods and wilderness, over bogs and great rivers. . . .

. . . We got over the river Delaware, not without great danger to . . . some of our lives. When we were over we were troubled to procure guides, which were hard to get, and very chargeable. Then had we that wilderness country, since called West Jersey, to pass through, not then inhabited by English; so that we sometimes traveled a whole day together without seeing man or woman, house or dwelling place. Sometimes we lay in the woods by a fire, and sometimes in the Indians' wigwams or houses.

We came one night to an Indian town, and lay at the house of the king, who was a very pretty [meaning kindly] man. Both he and his wife received us very lovingly, and his attendants (such as they were) were very respectful to us. They gave us mats to lie on; but provision was very short with them, they having caught but little that day. At another Indian town where we stayed, the king came to us, and he could speak some English. I spoke to him much, and also to his people; and they were very loving to us.

At length we came to Middletown, an English plantation in East Jersey, and there we found some Friends; but we could not stay to have a meeting at that time, being earnestly pressed in our spirits to get to the half-year's meeting of Friends at Oyster Bay, in Long Island, which was very near at hand. . . .

The half-year's meeting began next day, which was the first day of the week, and lasted four days. The first and second days we had public meetings for worship, to which people of all sorts came; on the third day were the men's and women's meetings, wherein the affairs of the Church were taken care of. Here we met with some bad spirits, who had run out from Truth into prejudice, contention, and opposition to the order of Truth. . . .

The men's and women's meetings being over, on the fourth day we had a meeting with these discontented people, to which as many of them as chose came, and as many Friends as desired were present also; and the Lord's power broke forth gloriously to the confounding of the gainsayers. Then some of those who . . . had been chief in the mischievous work of contention and opposition against the Truth began to fawn upon me, and to cast the blame upon others; but the deceitful spirit was judged down and condemned, and the glorious Truth of

God was exalted and set over all; and they were all brought down and bowed under. Which was of great service to Truth, and to the satisfaction and comfort of Friends; glory to the Lord forever!

. . . We next returned to Oyster Bay, waiting for a wind to carry us to Rhode Island, which was computed to be about two hundred miles. As soon as the wind served, we set sail. We arrived there on the thirtieth day of the Third month, and were gladly received by Friends. We went to the house of Nicholas Easton, who at that time was governor of the island; where we rested, being very weary with traveling.

On First-day following we had a large meeting, to which came the deputy governor and several justices, who were mightily affected with the Truth. The week following, the Yearly Meeting for all the Friends of New England and the other colonies adjacent, was held in this island. . . .

This meeting lasted six days, the first four days being general public meetings for worship, to which abundance of other people came. . . . They having no priest in the island, and so no restriction to any particular way of worship; and both the governor and deputy governor, with several justices of the peace, daily frequented the meetings; this so encouraged the people that they flocked in from all parts of the island. Very good service we had amongst them, and Truth had good reception. . . .

These public meetings over, the men's meeting began, which was large, precious, and weighty. The day following was the women's meeting, which also was large and very solemn. These two meetings being for ordering the affairs of the Church, many weighty things were opened, and communicated . . . by way of advice, information, and instruction in the services relating thereunto; that all might be kept clean, sweet and savory amongst them. In these, several men's and women's meetings for other parts were agreed and settled, to take care of the poor, and other affairs of the Church, and to see that all who profess Truth walk according to the glorious gospel of God.

When this great general meeting was ended, it was somewhat hard for Friends to part; for the glorious power of the Lord, which was over all, and His Blessed Truth and life flowing amongst them, had so knit and united them together, that they spent two days in taking leave one of another, and of the Friends of the island; and then, being mightily filled with the presence and power of the Lord, they went away with joyful hearts to their several habitations, in the several colonies where they lived. . . .

After this I had a great travail in spirit concerning the Ranters in those parts, who had been rude at a meeting at which I was not present. Wherefore I appointed a meeting amongst them, believing the Lord would give me power over them; which He did, to His praise and glory; blessed be His name forever! There were at this meeting many Friends, and diverse other people; some of whom were justices of the peace, and officers, who were generally well affected with the Truth. One, who had been a justice twenty years, was convinced, spoke highly of the Truth, and more highly of me than is fit for me to mention or take notice of. . . .

I went thence towards Shelter Island. . . .* We went in a sloop; and passing by . . . Block Island, we came to Fisher's Island, where at night we went on shore; but were not able to stay for the mosquitoes which abound there, and are very troublesome. Therefore we went into our sloop again, put off for the shore, and cast anchor; and so lay in our sloop that night.

Next day we went into the Sound, but finding our sloop was not able to live in that water, we returned again, and came to anchor before Fisher's Island, where we lay in our sloop that night also. There fell abundance of rain, and our sloop being open, we were exceedingly wet.

Next day we passed over the waters called the Two Horse Races, and then by Gardner's Island; after which we passed by the Gull's Island, and so got at length to Shelter Island. Though it was but about twenty-seven

---

* Shelter Island, located at the Eastern end of Long Island, had been established as a shelter for persecuted Friends, hence the name Shelter.

leagues from Rhode Island, yet through the difficulty of passage we were three days in reaching it.

The day after, being First-day, we had a meeting there. In the same week I had another among the Indians; at which were their king, his council, and about a hundred Indians more. They sat down like Friends, and heard very attentively while I spoke to them by an interpreter, an Indian who . . . could speak English well. After the meeting they appeared very loving, and confessed that what was said to them was Truth. . . .

We stayed not long in Shelter Island, but entering our sloop again put to sea for Long Island. . . . We were upon the water all that day and the night following; but found ourselves next day driven back near to Fisher's Island. For there was a great fog, and towards day it was very dark, so that we could not see what way we made. Besides, it rained much in the night, which in our open sloop made us very wet. . . . Then we crossed the Sound, being all very wet; and much difficulty we had to get to land, the wind being strong against us. But blessed be the Lord God of heaven and earth, and of the seas and waters, all was well. . . .

While we were on this journey . . . , an accident befell, which for the time was a great exercise to us. John Jay, a Friend of Barbados, who had come with us from Rhode Island, and intended to accompany us through the woods to Maryland, being to try a horse, got upon his back, and the horse fell a-running, cast him down upon his head, and broke his neck, as the people said. Those that were near him took him up as dead, carried him a good way, and laid him on a tree.

I got to him as soon as I could; and, feeling him, concluded he was dead. As I stood pitying him and his family, I took hold of his hair, and his head turned any way, his neck was so limber. Whereupon I took his head in both my hands, and, setting my knees against the tree, I raised his head, and perceived there was nothing out or broken that way.

Then I put one hand under his chin, and the other behind his head, and raised his head two or three times with all my strength, and brought it in. I soon perceived his neck began to grow stiff again, and then he began to rattle in his throat, and quickly after to breathe.

The people were amazed; but I bade them have a good heart, be of good faith, and carry him into the house. They did so, and set him by the fire. I bade them get him something warm to drink, and put him to bed. After he had been in the house awhile he began to speak; but did not know where he had been. . . .

The next day we passed over a desperate river,* which had in it many rocks and broad stones, very hazardous to us and our horses. Thence we came to Christiana River, where we swam over our horses, and went over ourselves

---

* Possibly the Brandywine.

in canoes; but the sides of this river were so bad and wiry, that some of the horses were almost laid up....

Next day we waded through Chester River, a very broad water, and afterwards passing through many bad bogs, lay that night also in the woods by a fire, not having gone above thirty miles that day. The day following we traveled hard, though we had some troublesome bogs in our way; we rode about fifty miles, and got safe that night to Robert Harwood's, at Miles River, in Maryland....

On the 10th of the Eighth month we went thence about thirty miles by water, passing by Crane's Island, Swan Island, and Kent Island, in very foul weather and much rain. Our boat being open, we were not only very much wet, but in great danger of being overset; insomuch that some thought we could not escape being cast away. But, blessed be God, we fared very well, and came safely to shore next morning....

Afterward ... we sailed about ten miles to the house of James Frizby, a justice of the peace, where, the 16th of the Eighth month, we had a very large meeting, at which, besides Friends, were some hundreds of people, it was supposed. Amongst them were several justices, captains, and the sheriff, with other persons of note.

A blessed heavenly meeting this was; a powerful, thundering testimony for Truth was borne therein; a great sense there was upon the people, and much brokenness and tenderness amongst them....

. . . We then hastened towards Carolina; yet had several meetings by the way. . . . Our way . . . grew worse, being much of it plashy and pretty full of great bogs and swamps; so that we were commonly wet to the knees, and lay abroad at nights in the woods by a fire. . . .

In Virginia, the Governor, with his wife, received us lovingly; but a doctor there would needs dispute with us. And truly his opposing us was of good service, giving occasion for the opening of many things to the people concerning the Light and Spirit of God, which he denied to be in everyone; and affirmed that it was not in the Indians.

Whereupon I called an Indian to us, and asked him whether when he lied, or did wrong to any one, there was not something in him that reproved him for it. He said there was such a thing in him, that did so reprove him; and he was ashamed when he had done wrong, or spoken wrong. So we shamed the doctor before the Governor and the people; insomuch that the poor man ran out so far that at length he would not own the Scriptures. . . .

Having visited the north part of Carolina, and made a little entrance for Truth upon the people there, we began to return towards Virginia. . . . Next morning our boat was sunk; but we got her up, mended her, and went away in her that day about twenty-four miles, the water being rough, and the winds high; but the great power of God was seen, in carrying us safe in that rotten boat.

Having finished what service lay upon us in Virginia, on the 30th we set sail in an open sloop for Maryland. But having a great storm, and being much wet, we were glad to get to shore before night; and, walking to a house at Willoughby Point, we got lodging there that night. The woman of the house was a widow, and a very tender person; she had never received Friends before; but she received us very kindly, and with tears in her eyes.

We returned to our boat in the morning, and hoisted our sail, getting forward as fast as we could. But towards evening, a storm rising, we had much ado to get to shore; and our boat being open, the water splashed often in, and sometimes over us, so that we were completely wet. Being got to land, we made a fire in the woods to warm and dry us, and there we lay all night, the wolves howling about us.

On the 1st of the Eleventh month we sailed again. The wind being against us, we made but little headway, and were fain to get to shore at Point Comfort, where yet we found but small comfort. For the weather was so cold that though we made a good fire in the woods to lie by, the water that we had brought for our use was frozen near the fireside. We made to sea again next day; but the wind being strong and against us, we advanced but little. We were glad to get to land again, and traveled about to find some house where we might buy provisions, for our store was spent.

That night, also, we lay in the woods; and so extremely cold was the weather, the wind blowing high, and the frost and snow being great, that it was hard for some of us to abide it. . . . We passed over Potomac River also, the winds being high, the water very rough, our sloop open, and the weather extremely cold; and had a meeting there also, where some people were convinced. When we parted thence, some of our company went amongst them. We next steered our course for Patuxent River. I sat at the helm the greater part of the day, and some of the night. About the first hour in the morning we reached James Preston's house, on Patuxent River. . . .

After this the cold grew so exceedingly sharp, the frost and snow so extreme, beyond what was usual in that country, that we could hardly endure it. Neither was it easy or safe to stir out; yet we got, with some difficulty, six miles through the snow to John Mayor's, where we met with some Friends come from New England, whom we had left there when we came away; and glad we were to see each other, after so long and tedious travels. . . .

The 27th of the Eleventh month we had a very precious meeting in a tobacco house. The next day we returned to James Preston's, about eighteen miles distant. When we came there, we found his house had been burnt to the ground the night before, through the carelessness of a maidservant; so we lay three nights on the ground by the fire, the weather being very cold.

We made an observation which was somewhat strange, but certainly true; that one day, in the midst of this cold weather, the wind turning into the south, it grew so hot that we could hardly bear the heat; and the next day and night, the wind chopping back into the north, we could hardly endure the cold.

Having traveled through most parts of that country, and visited most of the plantations, and having sounded the alarm to all people where we came, and proclaimed the day of God's salvation amongst them, we found our spirits began to be clear of these parts of the world, and draw towards Old England again. . . .

. . . The 21st of the Third month, 1673, we set sail for England; the same day Richard Covell came on board our ship, having had his own taken from him by the Dutch.

We had foul weather and contrary winds, which caused us to cast anchor often, so that it was . . . the 31st ere we could get past the capes of Virginia and out into the main sea. But after this we made good speed, and on the 28th of the Fourth month cast anchor at King's Road, which is the harbor for Bristol.

We had on our passage very high winds and tempestuous weather, which made the sea exceedingly rough, the waves rising like mountains; so that the masters and sailors wondered at it, and said they had never seen the like before. But though the wind was strong it set for the most part with us, so that we sailed before it; and the great God who commands the winds, who is Lord of heaven, of earth, and the seas, and whose wonders are seen in the deep, steered our course and preserved us from many imminent dangers. The same good hand of Providence that went with us, and carried us safely over, watched over us in our return, and brought us safely back again; thanksgiving and praises be to his holy name forever!

Many sweet and precious meetings we had on board the ship during this voyage (commonly two a week), wherein the blessed presence of the Lord did greatly refresh us, and often break in upon and tender the company.

When we came into Bristol harbor, there lay a man-of-war, and the press master came on board to impress our men. We had a meeting at that time in the ship with the seamen, before we went to shore; and the press master sat down with us, stayed the meeting, and was well satisfied with it. After the meeting I spoke to him to leave in our ship two of the men he had impressed, for he had impressed four, one of whom was a lame man. He said, "At your request I will." . . .

Chapter Nineteen

The Last Imprisonment
(1673–1678)

I PASSED INTO WILTSHIRE, where also we had many blessed meetings. At Slattenford, in Wiltshire, we had a very good meeting, though we met there with much opposition from some who had set themselves against women's meetings;* which I was moved of the Lord to recommend to Friends, for the benefit and advantage of the Church of Christ, "that faithful women, who were called to the belief of the Truth, being made partakers of the same precious faith, and heirs of the same everlasting gospel

---

* This became a major controversy within the Friends and led to much conflict and trouble for Fox.

of life and salvation with the men, might in like manner come into the possession and practice of the gospel order, and therein be helpmeets unto the men in the restoration of those fallen away in the service of Truth, in the affairs of the Church, as they are outwardly in civil, or temporal things." . . .

[After a visit with William Penn at the latter's home at Rickmansworth, he started on his journey north towards Swarthmore, accompanied by his wife, two of her daughters and his son-in-law, Thomas Lower, a journey which led to more than a year's imprisonment—his last imprisonment, as it proved.] . . .

After over a year's imprisonment . . . my wife went to London on about October 1, 1674, and spoke to the King, laying before him my long and unjust imprisonment, . . . the manner of my being taken, and the justices' proceedings against me, in tendering me the oath as a snare, whereby they had praemunired me; so that I being now his prisoner, it was in his power, and at his pleasure, to release me, which she desired.

The King spoke kindly to her, and referred her to the Lord Keeper; to whom she went; but she could not obtain what she desired, for he said the King could not release me otherwise than by a pardon, and I was not free to receive a pardon, knowing I had not done evil. If I would have been freed by a pardon, I need not have lain so long, for the King was willing to give me pardon long before, and told Thomas Moore that I need not scruple, being released by a pardon, for many a man that was as innocent as a child had had a pardon granted him; yet I could not consent to have one. For I would rather have lain in prison all my days, than have come out in any way dishonorable to Truth; therefore I chose to have the validity of my indictment tried before the judges. . . .

We came to London on the 8th, and on the 11th I was brought before the four judges at the King's Bench, where Counselor Corbet pleaded my cause. . . .

The next day they chose . . . to . . . begin with the . . . indictment; and when they came to be opened, they were so many and gross that the judges were all of opinion that the indictment was quashed and void, and that I ought to have my liberty.

There were that day several great men, lords and others, who had the oaths of allegiance and supremacy tendered to them in open court, just before my trial came on; and some of my adversaries moved the judges that the oaths might be tendered again to me, telling them I was a dangerous man to be at liberty.

But Chief Justice Hale said that he had indeed heard some such reports, but he had also heard many more good reports of me; and so he and the rest of the judges ordered me to be freed by proclamation.

Thus after I had suffered imprisonment a year and almost two months for nothing, I was fairly set at liberty upon a trial of the errors in my indictment, without receiving any pardon, or coming under any obligation ... and the Lord's everlasting power went over all, to His glory and praise. ...

Being at liberty, I visited Friends in London; and having been very weak, and not yet well recovered,* I went to Kingston; and having visited Friends there, returned to London, wrote a paper to the Parliament, and sent several books to them.

A great book against swearing [having to take oaths] had been delivered to them a little before; the reasonableness whereof had so much influence, that it was thought they would have done something towards our relief if they had sat longer. I stayed in and near London till the yearly meeting, to which Friends came from most parts of the nation, and some from beyond the sea. A glorious meeting we had in the everlasting power of God.

The illness I got in my imprisonment at Worcester had so much weakened me that it was long before I recovered my natural strength again. For which reason, and as many things lay upon me to write, both for public and private service, I did not stir much abroad during the time that I now stayed in the north; but when Friends were not with me, I spent much time in writing for Truth's service. While I was at Swarthmore, I gave several books to be printed. ...

---

* Fox, at 5 1, was much weakened, although he would live 1 4 years more.

After the yearly meeting, having stayed a week or two with Friends in London, I went down with William Penn to his house in Sussex, . . . Worminghurst, for about three weeks; in which time John Burnyeat and I answered a very envious and wicked book, which Roger Williams, a priest of New England (or some colony thereabouts) had written against Truth and Friends. . . .*

Thence we went to Kingston, and so to London, where I stayed not long; for it was upon me from the Lord to go into Holland, to visit Friends and to preach the gospel there, and in some parts of Germany. . . .

---

* Fox had missed meeting Roger Williams, the governor of Rhode Island, while in that colony. Williams's attack was entitled "George Fox Digged Out of His Burrows."

The Testimony of William Penn* concerning that Faithful Servant George Fox

This George Fox was born in Leicestershire, about the year 1624....

... As to his employment, he was brought up in country business; and as he took most delight in sheep, so he was very skillful in them; an employment that very well suited his mind in several respects, both for its innocence and solitude....

... When he was somewhat above twenty, he left his friends, and visited the most retired and religious people, and some there were at that time in this nation, especially in those parts, who waited for

* Founder of the American Colony Pennsylvania, later an important state of The United States and location of its first Capitol.

the consolation of Israel night and day, as Zacharias, Anna, and good old Simeon did of old time. . . .

In 1652, age 28, he being in his usual retirement to the Lord upon a very high mountain, in some of the hither parts of Yorkshire, . . . he had a vision of the great work of God in the earth, and of the way that he was to go forth to begin it. . . .

. . . Through the tender and singular indulgence of Judge Bradshaw and Judge Fell, in the infancy of things, the priests of the government sanctioned and supported Anglican or Presbyterian churches were never able to gain the point they labored for, which was to have proceeded to blood, and if possible, Herod-like, by a cruel exercise of the civil power, to have cut Fox and his followers . . . off and rooted them out of the country. . . .

Fox's . . . ministry and writings show they are from one that was not taught of man, nor had learned what he said by study. . . .

. . . The most awful, living, reverent frame I ever felt or beheld, I must say, was his in prayer. . . .

. . . He was so meek, contented, modest, easy, steady, tender, it was a pleasure to be in his company. . . . A most merciful man, he was as ready to forgive as unapt to take or give offense. . . .

. . . Towards the conclusion of his traveling services, between age . . . seventy-one and seventy-seven, he visited the churches of Christ in the plantations in America, and in the United Provinces, and Germany, as his . . . Journal relates, to the convincement and consolation of many. . . .

. . . I give my . . . report of him, and my witness is true, having been with him for weeks and months together on diverse occasions, and those of the . . . most exercising nature . . . by night and by day, by sea and by land, in this and in foreign countries. I can say I never saw him out of his place or not a match for every service or occasion. . . .

. . . He was also . . . civil beyond all forms of breeding in his behavior very temperate, eating little and sleeping less, though a bulky person. . .

Index

ς